MOOSHIE

ALSO BY ECHO HERON

NONFICTION
INTENSIVE CARE: The Story of a Nurse
CONDITION CRITICAL: The Story of a Nurse Continues
TENDING LIVES: Nurses on the Medical Front
EMERGENCY 24/7: Nurses of the Emergency Room

FICTION
MERCY: A Medical Novel
NOON AT TIFFANY'S: An Historical, Biographical Novel

MYSTERIES
The Adele Monsarrat Medical Mystery series:
PULSE
PANIC
PARADOX
FATAL DIAGNOSIS

MOOSHIE

LIFE WITH AN UNCONVENTIONAL CAT

ECHO HERON

HERON
QUILL
PRESS

2021

Published in the United States by Heron Quill Press, LLC

MOOSHIE
Life With an Unconventional Cat

ISBN: 978-1-938439-84-1

http://www.echoheron

Front cover photo: Joni Frasson
Back cover photos: Echo Heron / Joni Frasson

AUTHOR'S NOTE

I have written this book to describe my experiences, thoughts, and feelings about life with my cat, Mooshie. Although Mooshie isn't here to meow and chirp for himself, I believe he would agree with the actions, thoughts, and feelings I have attributed to him.

The events herein took place two and three decades ago. While the incidents I describe are based on actual occurrences, some of the chronology and locations have been altered. In certain instances I have taken creative license for narrative purposes, and supplemented the dialogue or actions consistent with the character or nature of the person speaking, and/or the events being described.

Except for a few individuals, (Simon, Dr. Joseph Thompson, Joni, Lindo, Robin Williams, Catherine, Janey) I have used fictitious names and identifying characteristics for other individuals portrayed in this work.

This book is not meant to focus criticism on any particular group, institution, place, or individual either living or dead. Any resemblances the reader may imagine they discern, are unintended and entirely coincidental.

In memory of Mooshie,
the finest cat I have ever loved

CONTENTS

PART FOUR
ANIMAL SHELTER

PART FIVE
RETIREMENT: A BLANKET OF ONE'S OWN

PREFACE

The relationship between cats and humans has always been complex, and at times confusing. Take, for instance, the question of ownership.

Contrary to popular belief, it is the cat who chooses its human, not the other way around. You may *think* you had a choice when you adopted your feline, but you did not. A cat knows long before the two of you meet exactly what type of human it will own. The cat may even recoil and hiss as you dip into the box or cage to pull it out, but this is simply feline melodrama—the animal has already put a spell on you and is merely playing hard to get.

The cat who owned me exclusively for fifteen years was more like a spouse than a pet. He was a far better friend to me than my best friend, and as much a child of mine as if I'd birthed him myself. Over the top you say? Just ask my ex-husband, my ex-best friend, and my son. They all freely admit they were jealous of us—the perfect interspecies couple.

His public knew him as Mooshie, although his formal registered name was Mushu Pork With Pancakes. He was a sable Burmese distinguished by a rounded head and protruding yellow-gold eyes. Some people who knew him personally thought he was my familiar—a gift direct from Satan's Warehouse. Still others, (I cast my vote with this group) insisted he was a failed insemination attempt between an alien and Yoda.

If I were to analyze this cat of mine, I'd say he possessed a deep understanding of the limitations of humans. Mooshie's capacity for love, along with his perceptive nature, made it easy for him to flow with the backwash of my many shortcomings. I believe he developed his Monty Pythonesque sense of humor and comedic timing as a way to divert humans' attention away from their troubles and on to him.

All cats are extraordinary; there is no denying that. Terry Pratchett famously wrote of cats: "In ancient times cats were worshiped as gods; they have not forgotten this." But every once in a while, a cat is born that is different from the rest—an unconventional cat, if you will.

Most of us have heard or read about the true-life accounts of stalwart cats that traveled thousands of miles to find their humans. Then there are those heroic cats that woke their humans out of a sound sleep to warn them of some life-threatening danger headed their way. And, there are the celebrity cats—Ernest Hemingway's Boise, Christopher Smart's Jeoffry, Cleveland Amory's Polar Bear, and Peter Gethers's Norton.

Heroics and fame aside, I suspect that the humans who admit they are owned by these animals, do so at first with reluctance for fear that no one will believe the traits and feats that make these cats remarkable. I have no such reluctance. Plainly put, Mooshie was an exceptional and unconventional cat. How he got that way is anyone's guess. Perhaps as the runt of the litter, he was forced to expand his intellect and reasoning powers in order to beat the fat cats to the teat and survive. Whatever it was that made him unique, his wonderfully quirky and intelligent nature worked to his advantage. The people into whose lives he crept will never forget him.

A literary agent once advised that if I wanted to see this book published, I would need to follow the standard pet book recipe: an animal suddenly appears, it helps lots of people solve their problems, and then it dies.

I can't claim that Mooshie suddenly appeared—I went out to find him. I can't say that he helped lots of people solve their problems, though he sure enriched *my* life. Sadly, I *can* say that he did die, but that wasn't the end of him—not by a long shot.

Mooshie has made brief appearances in several of my previous books, but a full-length nuzzle-and-tell book about my unconventional cat and our entertaining and adventurous life together?

Well, that's another story—this one.

Echo Heron
San Francisco, 2021

cat: / kat /
noun
a small carnivorous mammal, valued by humans for its companionship and its ability to hunt vermin. It has been associated with humans for at least 9,500 years. A skilled predator, the cat is intelligent and can be trained to obey simple commands. Individual cats have also been known to have the ability to manipulate simple mechanisms. Cats use a variety of vocalizations and body language for communication, including mewing ("meow" or "miaow"), purring, hissing, tail swishing, growling, squeaking, ear twitching, chirping, clicking, and grunting.

unconventional: / enken'ven(t)SH(e)n(e)l /
adjective
someone or something that deviates from the norm or accepted standard: not bound by, or conforming to what is generally done or believed; to exist out of the bounds of cultural norms; an outlier.

PART ONE

THE FORMATIVE YEARS

· I ·

THE CHOSEN

"But if you tame me, then we shall need each other.
To me, you will be unique in all the world. To you,
I shall be unique in all the world."
— Antoine de Saint-Exupéry, *The Little Prince*

On Mother's Day 1984, I was on a mission that, unbeknownst to me, would change the course of my life. With my thirteen-year-old son Simon riding shotgun, and yours truly behind the wheel of our 1957 Chevy station wagon, we headed south of San Francisco through the miles of urban sprawl, every inch of it blighted by freeways and boxy houses built atop one another. As I cruised blithely through the smog, I mulled over what I'd learned about the object of this expedition—a Burmese cat.

As the story goes, in 1930 a promiscuous female looking for love stowed away on an American Naval ship docked in Burma. The Burmese floozy chose just the right vessel because the sailors, eager for a little female companionship, took her in and fell in love.

The diminutive heartbreaker was doted on, loved up, and fussed over, all the way back to San Francisco Bay where she was handed over to retired Navy physician-turned-cat-breeder, Joseph Thompson. Dr. Thompson christened the Burmese coquette, Wong Mau, introduced her to several Siamese studs and gave her the job she was heatedly seeking. The result of Wong Mau's labors was a compact breed marked by enormous yellow bug-eyes and an intelligent and mischievous nature.

Burmese cats have many outstanding qualities, but there were two that I found particularly appealing. The first was a matter of practicality: Burmese cats are excellent mousers, which provided the perfect eradication solution to the king-sized Norwegian wharf rats that routinely invaded our creekside cottage.

The most important draw, and the trait that made a Burmese my "must-have" cat, was that they are, by nature, the most devoted and affectionate of felines. This was just what my therapist ordered—a loving, nonjudgmental, mutually respectful, and uncomplicated relationship with a loyal, long-term companion.

Straight men in my age range who were looking for a committed relationship were in extremely short supply. Nonetheless, all my married friends wanted me to be married too. Though they meant well, the unsuitable blind dates they insisted on setting me up with made the prospect of spinsterhood increasingly attractive.

Furthermore, Simon had recently deemed it

developmentally appropriate that he should spend at least 50 percent of his time with his father doing "guy stuff," which placed me in the half-empty nester category.

My writing and running habits were also detrimental to finding a partner. I devoted a good deal of my time to writing—a lifelong passion that could be either torturous or exhilarating depending on the day. I'd had a couple of stories published in *Reader's Digest,* and was hoping that writing would morph into a second career.

The problem lay in the fact that writing is something one does alone in a secluded environment. The chances that I'd meet new people and make friends or romantic connections were slim to none—unless they showed up at my door. And since I wasn't into Jehovah's Witnesses or the mailman, I was out of luck.

Being a devoted runner, I was pretty sure that connecting with someone on backwoods trails while running at six miles per hour was never going to happen either.

Then there was my career as a registered nurse in the emergency room and acute coronary care unit of the local hospital. Permanently assigned to the inappropriately dubbed "swing" shift—three to eleven thirty p.m.—I was usually up to my eyeballs in the chaos of other people's life and death struggles when most humans were out in the world socializing.

I'll admit I wasn't *entirely* alone. I did have the company of Perch And Twirl, a sweet German Roller Canary that one of my untrue loves bestowed upon me the day he left

3

me for a man he met inside a Judy Garland blow-up costume at the San Francisco Gay Pride parade. Ever try cuddling up with a small bird after you've had a lousy day and are hoping to get a little sympathy? Snails would be more receptive.

On the positive side, I had a long history with cats. A cat lover from the cradle, my first spoken words were neither mama nor dada, but rather, "kitty meow." My first constant companion was a stuffed toy kitten that could always be found on or near my person until I entered the first grade. Though we didn't have a family cat, I was seven when the neighborhood kids (way ahead of their time) christened me "The Crazy Cat Lady." I was the village go-to person for anyone who needed a cat sitter, and the dedicated depositary for an endless string of strays.

In my young adult years, a few cats tempted me to bring them into my life, but I was always too busy or too much on the move to give them the attention they deserved.

All my instincts pushed me to the conclusion that I would never be complete without a cat. Bringing a forever cat into my life was a sure bet for happiness and the perfect twofold solution to my desire for a loving companion— and the rats. Besides, whoever heard of a writer without a cat?

*

The cat breeder's house was in a crowded subdivision where the streets were laid out in a complex maze of identical cookie-cutter houses. In true California style,

4

house numbers were cleverly hidden under eaves, behind dense bushes, or simply not displayed. We drove around for a solid forty-five minutes—sometimes in circles, sometimes into dead ends—all without seeing another human being or vehicle. It was like being caught in an episode of *The Twilight Zone,* traveling through another dimension. Each time I turned onto another deserted street, I half expected to see Rod Serling waiting for us.

Fearful that we would be trapped forever in this eerie labyrinth, I was beginning to feel claustrophobic when we spotted a house displaying a half dozen pink plastic flamingos staked into the white gravel front yard. In a bizarre David Lynchian twist, ceramic kittens had been wired into place around the neck of each bird.

Sure that we had reached our destination, we headed for the porch. We'd only gone a few steps when we were assaulted by an invisible wall of malodorous cat spray. We held our breath and rushed to the door, where our attention was diverted by the dozen or so plaques displaying a variety of hackneyed phrases such as *Cats are God's children with fur,* and, *All cats are purrrfect!* It was upon hearing the doorbell play *The Farmer in the Dell* in cute chime tones, that my mission to purchase a cat from this house turned into an animal rescue operation.

The door was opened by a woman whose appearance left me momentarily mute. Imagine if you will, a zaftig, middle-aged woman wearing straight-cut Mamie Eisenhower bangs, bright red lipstick, and purple cat frame glasses. The front of her pink sweatshirt was emblazoned with a cartoon cat face that featured huge green rhinestones for eyes. In jarring contrast to the flashy top, her capri pants were geometrically patterned with black and white cat heads. Dangling Sylvester the Cat earrings capped the woman's thought-provoking fashion choices.

Identifying herself as "Betty the Breeder," she led us to a living room right out of a Diane Arbus photo album on Americana—lime green shag carpets, an overabundance of ceramic cat knickknacks, a Sears furniture collection circa 1951, and a color TV sitting shrine-like in the corner. Strategically placed in front of the screen was a rocking chair occupied by an elderly woman who was introduced to us as, "My mother who is visiting for a *short* time."

We settled ourselves on the plastic-encased sofa while Betty the Breeder gathered a kindle of roaming Abyssinian kittens, and placed them into a sizable cage on wheels.

"I have to lock the Abbys in before I set the Burms loose. The two breeds must be kept separate for reasons of"—Betty lowered her voice—"interbreeding."

Betty reappeared ten minutes later, each side of her body draped in squirming sable kittens with huge yellow eyes. The instant their paws hit the floor they were on the move: running and leaping from tables to shelves, shelves to chairs. Mostly, they made a run for the old lady in the rocking chair, covering her like so many chocolate sprinkles. One sat on her shoulder, while another hung from the bun at the nape of her neck. A few wiggled down the front of her dress. Several others used her support stockings as assistive climbing devices.

Not wanting to crush or maim one of the product lines, the old lady stopped rocking and began picking kittens off her clothes like one might pick cockleburs off a sweater. "God, I hate cats!"

I smiled uncertainly. "You're joking."

Her steely blue eyes narrowed. "I'm serious as a heart attack. I can't stand these sneaky little bastards. Hated 'em since I was a kid. I'm a dog person to the core. I disowned my daughter fifteen years ago when she started cat-trading. I only visit once a year on Mother's Day for appearance's sake."

The old lady leaned in close. "How about a nice mastiff?" she whispered. "I'm a certified dog trader. Maybe you and the boy want to rethink this; get your boy a dog instead of one of these prissy weasels."

"Mother!" Betty unceremoniously yanked the old lady to her feet. "Go take a nap."

Rolling her eyes, the old woman scraped the rest of the kittens from her clothes. Executing a crisp military salute, she turned and hobbled down the hall, one kitten still hanging off the back of her sweater.

The breeder sat facing me. Knee-to-knee, she fixed me with a flinty stare. "I hope you don't have plans to travel any time soon."

Knowing that new kittens should not be left alone for the first few days after adoption, I smiled. "No worries— I've taken two weeks off. After I return to work, my son will be there after school to make sure the kitten is—"

Lips pursed, Betty adjusted her glasses. "I'm afraid you

don't understand. Let me explain the Burmese nature. When I say I hope you don't have travel plans, I mean for the next fifteen to twenty *years.* You cannot be owned by a Burmese and think you're going to be taking vacations too. Have you ever known anyone owned by a Burmese?"

Her odd phraseology gave me pause. "Well, my cousin owns a Burmese and she says—"

"Your cousin does not *own* a Burmese, dear. The Burmese owns *her.*" The breeder rearranged her mouth in a patronizing smile. "You see, in the cat world Burmese are known as the People Cats. They've been bred to bond with one, and on a rare occasion, two, people for life."

"Sounds pretty codependent to me," I jested, hoping to interject a note of levity.

The breeder frowned. "It's no laughing matter I assure you. Burmese are like clingy boyfriends. The usual feline independent nature has been bred out of them. If you have a job that requires you to be away from home, or if you take vacations that last longer than two or three days, you would be better off looking at another breed—Abyssinians, for instance. Abbys are more independent and slightly aloof."

Properly sobered, I took on an expression I might have worn to the funeral of a dear friend. "Well, I don't travel for a living, and I—"

A scrawny runt straddled my shoulder and studiously sniffed my hair. Three other kittens were making their way up my legs.

"—I haven't taken a real vacation in years, although I—"

"Good, because if these cats are separated from their

primary human for longer than a few days, they will cease to thrive."

Betty searched through the mob of felines, found the kitten she wanted, and shoved the animal into my hands. "This is the cat for you! He *is* a factory second, so I'll let you have him for a greatly reduced price—only two hundred ninety-five dollars."

Mindful that the kitten was hissing and trying to sink its teeth into my wrist, I handed it back to the breeder. It was only then that I noticed the last part of its tail was bent at a sharp angle.

"We don't know how the tail thing happened," Betty was quick to tell me. "His lineage is excellent as you can see from the perfectly round shape of his skull and the protuberance of the eyes. If it wasn't for his"—she made air quotes—"*deformity*, he'd be show quality."

There was a soft tap on the side of my head. I turned and came nose-to-nose with the scruffy sable runt that had been sniffing my hair. He looked into my eyes in a meaningful way, pawed my nose, and then sat back to wait. As I held his gaze, I experienced a strong sense of recognition.

Betty reclaimed my attention by shoving Hook Tail back into my arms. Sensing competition, the runt found my earlobe and commenced suckling. I gently broke suction and continued listening to the breeder go on about how I could, if I so desired, turn Hook Tail into a faux Manx Burmese.

The runt wiggled his behind and leaped, landing on

Simon's shoulder without a wobble. Had it been a precision landing competition, Runt Boy would have taken the gold.

Simon didn't flinch; he had his eye on Runt Boy as well.

The breeder's canned lecture about *Defective Cats and What Wonderful Pets They Make* was completely lost on us. Our attention was again captured by the feline Flying Wallenda as he moved from Simon's shoulder to his head, where he perched like a bird.

I was about to get up to take a closer look at the imp when he again hurtled through the air and made a perfect landing on my shoulder. He pawed my cheek, waited for me to face him, then leaned forward and attached himself to the end of my nose using his tiny needle-sharp teeth. The kitten's message was clear: *You have been chosen. Now get me out of this hellhole!*

A ripple of emotion went through me as goosebumps covered my arms. I pried the runt off my nose and studied his sweet face. I felt deeply honored, as if a god had selected me to be his personal assistant.

I glanced over at Simon, who nodded his approval.

"We want this one," I blurted.

Betty, who was still going on about Hook Tail's positive attributes, faltered and glanced at the kitten I held in my hand. "Oh no, no, no, no. I'm afraid I can't let you have that one, dear. Besides, he's only pet quality. This one is show quality and despite that tail, he will make a much better pet in the long run."

"*Why* can't we have this one?" I asked, trying to ignore Runt Boy, who had found his way inside my blouse.

10

The breeder pursed her lips. "He's only fourteen weeks old. He's not yet fully weaned."

She wasn't lying about that—the animal was tearing at my bra, frantically trying to suckle my nipple through the nylon. I pressed my case.

"Surely at three and a half months he can switch over to solid food?"

The breeder took on the expression of a disapproving schoolmarm. "You don't know what you're getting into. He's the runt, and it's a well-known fact that runts are feline-challenged. You'll be saddled with a misfit cat for as long as he's alive."

At the time I had no idea how to interpret "feline-challenged," or "misfit cat," but feeling optimistic, I waved her warnings aside.

She pointed at the moving lump under my blouse. "He has other problems as well. Physical problems."

"What other physical problems?"

The breeder sniffed. "His adult teeth are coming in and it appears one of his canines is quite a bit longer than the other. You don't want a cat with a malformed mouth."

"How much longer is it?" I was growing impatient.

"At present only a millimeter, but it could grow longer by as much as two to three millimeters. He'll look hideous. People will call him Snaggletooth or Fang."

I was hardly able to contain my irritation. If this breeder thought the kitten was too damaged to be salable on the strength of one tooth being a millimeter too long, what was going to happen to him? For that matter, what had happened to the other kittens that had slight flaws?

My polite and patient demeanor vanished. "Since when is a millimeter of tooth enamel considered a malformed mouth?"

Betty the Breeder must have missed the anger behind my question because she continued disqualifying Runt Boy as a contender.

"A runt with a malformed mouth isn't fit to be—"

I abruptly got to my feet, making sure to hold onto Runt Boy, who was still hiding under my blouse. "I don't care. We want this kitten. How much longer before you'll release him?"

Betty's mouth went into a tight thin line of disapproval. "I can't possibly let him go for at least two or three more months."

This was confusing, considering that the woman had just told me how deficient Runt Boy was. I'd read that breeders sometimes held onto kittens until they could determine if the cat was of show, champion, or breeding quality. That could mean anywhere from four to six months. The idea of taking on a cat whose personality had been shaped by this breeder's chaotic household brought the words "institutionalized animal" to mind.

I sighed, shook my head, and removed Runt Boy from inside my blouse. He bestowed upon me a glorious bright-eyed smile and chirped. It was at that precise moment that I fell madly, profoundly in love. It sounds corny, but my soul—which as of late had been crouching in some dark and moldy corners—opened and sucked in fresh, sunshine-saturated air. Our bond was forged. It was clear that Runt Boy was not going to endure another two months without me, nor I without him.

"I'm sorry, but I don't want to wait that long, nor do I care to make that drive again. I want a young kitten, one that will be free to develop his own unique personality in a loving home."

Taking a gamble, I put Runt Boy down on the back of the couch. He mewled piteously, his crestfallen expression uncannily human-like. I came close to losing it right then and there, but I was sure that if I could play the role a little longer, Betty would crack like a thin-shelled egg.

I rearranged my face into the best businesswoman-of-steel expression I could muster. "Perhaps you know of someone closer to Marin who has Burmese kittens they'd be willing to part with now?"

Seeing two hundred and fifty dollars get up from the couch and walk away, Betty bolted to the front door, blocking my way. Panic was in her eyes as she looked from me to Runt Boy, who had crawled inside my purse and was busy making a nest for himself between my checkbook and my stethoscope.

"I suppose I could break the rules this once," she grumbled. "But if the Burmese Breeders Society hears about this, I'll lose my license."

I reached for my checkbook. "I won't tell if you don't."

Runt Boy licked the back of my hand as I wrote out a check that equaled a good portion of my weekly salary.

My check securely tucked away in her ample cleavage,

Betty spent the next fifteen minutes going over the ten pages of certifications, rules, and operating instructions that came with the animal. We were then formally introduced to Irish Coffee, Runt Boy's handsome bull-necked sire. Irish Coffee presented his offspring with an impromptu farewell christening by spraying my purse. Runt Boy's mother, Tootsie Roll, embarrassed at having produced a scruffy, snaggletoothed runt, refused to leave her current litter of champions and showstoppers.

After issuing a final warning about a Burmese's dependency on its human, the breeder handed over Runt Boy's birth certificate, vaccination schedule, and a sample bag of kitten kibble. She ushered us out with a promise that once we settled on a name, she would send Runt Boy's certified registration papers in the mail.

I set my purse carefully on the backseat and gazed down at our precious new bundle snoozing at the bottom. I felt such a surge of maternal love for the helpless thing, that for a moment, I felt phantom breast ache with the letdown of non-existent milk. Snapping back to reality, I slipped behind the wheel of the Chevy and left the House of Feline Detention behind.

His first yowls of distress pierced the air as we were passing through Berkeley. Worried that the kitten might have stabbed himself with a pencil or a nail file, I pulled over, dug him out of my bag, and moved my fingers over his little body, searching for injury. I found no wounds, but in the full light of day, Runt Boy appeared to be little more than a malnourished bag of bones covered in spiky shreds of matted brown fuzz that resembled a moth-eaten toupee.

"Maybe he's hungry," Simon suggested, opening the sample bag of kibble.

Before Simon had time to withdraw his hand, Runt Boy attacked the bag, his baby teeth bared and his eyes wide. He ravenously wolfed down the pellets, simultaneously making a drawn-out, high-pitched warbling growl that was eerily similar to the sound of mating raccoons.

Thinking of the Holocaust survivors, I was sure he'd get sick if he ate too much all at once. I tried pulling the bag away, but he threw himself over it, holding on like it was a life raft in stormy seas. I visually inspected him as he inhaled the food. The prominence of his ribs and hipbones and the hollows around his buggy eyes brought the reality of the kitten's condition home. Unintentional as it may have been, the animal was literally starving.

"My God," I whispered, "he's like a poster cat for UNICEF."

Sympathetic to the kitten's plight, Simon reached over to stroke his head. Mistaking the gesture as intent to steal his food, Runt Boy sank his teeth deep into Simon's finger. Screams from both kitten and boy filled the car.

His snaggletooth still engaged with Simon's right index finger, the kitten hung on. Pale and clammy, Simon went silent. I seized the squirming feline by the back of his skull and carefully disengaged his teeth from my son's finger. In a classic display of food insecurity, Runt Boy backed into the cargo hold of the Chevy dragging the bag of kibbles with him.

On our way to the nearest walk-in clinic, I glanced into the rearview mirror to see Runt Boy ravenously licking the inside of the empty cellophane bag. Runt Boy had been in our possession for only thirty minutes and already mayhem was afoot. I briefly questioned the wisdom of my choice and rationalized that any starved animal would turn Cujo-ish at the smell of food.

Once Simon's finger was X-rayed, cleaned, and bandaged, we returned to the car. Runt Boy was nowhere to be seen, but his muffled cries for help could be heard. Using my special echolocation technique, I concluded that Runt Boy was stuck somewhere inside the rear bench seat. I tried pushing my hand down the narrow opening between the seat and the backrest without luck.

Simon cradled his bandaged hand protectively to his chest and voted for leaving Runt Boy where he was. I might have considered that option, but those desolate howls clawed at my maternal instincts.

Lucky for us there was a body shop not far from the clinic. Twenty-five dollars went to the mechanic who removed the seat, extracted the animal, and bolted the seat back into place. From the body shop, we drove directly to a pet shop and stocked up on tins of the pricey organic kitten food guaranteed to make a kitten's fur, teeth, and bones strong and beautiful. I looked at Runt Boy's matted fuzz, snaggletooth, and jutting ribs and hoped the cat food was up to the task.

Within minutes of arriving home, I emptied a tin of cat food onto a saucer, put Runt Boy down next to it, and got out of biting range. The kitten climbed onto the plate, embraced the sides between his forelegs, and wolfed down the entire contents of the tin in thirty seconds flat. I didn't know whether to be amazed, amused, or horrified.

I opened a second tin but spooned only half of it into his bowl. This time the baby glutton slowed down enough to work the food over before swallowing. By the time he'd finished, Runt Boy resembled a boa constrictor digesting a small hot air balloon. He waddled two steps and fell, staying where he landed so as not to leave the food bowl unguarded. The clever beast's last action before he nodded off was to stretch out a paw and rest it on the bowl's rim— the feline version of food surveillance.

We sat down to our own dinner of Chinese takeout, both of us keeping an eye on the brown lump of fur.

"What should we name him?" Simon asked. "I kinda like Runt Boy."

"I don't think Runt Boy is politically correct. That would be like calling a vertically challenged person Shorty or Stumpy."

Simon gingerly touched his bandages. "How about Vicious Biter Boy?"

"Negative. That might give him a complex. What about Buster Brown?"

Simon looked puzzled.

"You know—from the Buster Brown shoe ads? The boy who lives in a shoe with his dog, Tige?"

Simon wiped away a dribble of pork sauce that had squirted out of its pancake and down the front of his shirt. "I think Brown Blood-Sucking Vampire is more like it, Mom."

I tucked into my Szechuan vegetables deluxe. "How about Buddha Boy? That might lead him to be an enlightened cat."

"I'd rather call him Buddha Boy's Brown Biting Butthole," Simon grumbled.

I snorted. "I don't think that would be—"

Out of nowhere, Runt Boy sprang onto Simon's back, his dinky needle-sharp claws firmly embedded into the sides of my son's neck. Arms flailing, Simon leaped out of his chair and flung himself about, trying to disengage his tormentor.

The kitten unhooked and landed unceremoniously in the middle of Simon's plate where he greedily polished off what remained of the mushu pork.

A trusting soul, Simon reached down to rescue his food.

By the time Simon's left index finger was cleaned and bandaged, the kitten had finished off Simon's pancake and eaten his way to the bottom of the takeout container.

Under our disbelieving, gobsmacked gazes, he slipped over to my vegetables deluxe, took one sniff, and scurried back into the Mushu pork takeout box. He went to work licking the remaining sauce off the inside walls.

"How about Glutton Boy?" Simon suggested. "It's simple and to the point."

I studied the small hind legs, rump, and scraggy tail issuing from the takeout box. On the outside of the container, someone had written:

MUSHU PORK w/ P.CAKES~TO GO

Easing the furry brown lump out from the food carton, I gently wiped him down using a damp towel. "How about Mushu Pork? We'll call him Mooshie for short."

Simon shrugged. "It's okay I guess, but don't you think it might make him nervous to have the same name as a Chinese menu item?"

*

Later that night I carried the newly-christened kitten to my bed and set him on the pillow that had been unemployed since my last boyfriend left to marry someone less like me, and more like himself.

The wheezy purr that blasted out of Mooshie's thin body made me laugh. I lay down next to him and pressed my finger to the pads of his front paw. He automatically stretched out both paws, wrapping them around the tip of my pinky—like a newborn grasping his mother's finger. That one endearing gesture left no question in my mind that ours was going to be a lifelong partnership.

I awoke hours later to the sound of loud manly-man snores. Disoriented, I thought perhaps my latest ex had returned, or that Simon had come in to see the kitten and fallen asleep. Except, this snore was the snore of a drunken, four-hundred-pound sumo wrestler.

I turned on the light. No ex-boyfriend, no Simon, no drunk sumo. It was Mooshie. I supposed it would take some getting used to, but I was a nurse—if I could get used to being puked, bled, peed, spat, and pooped on, I could handle cat snores.

The next morning I visited a Mommy and Me secondhand shop and purchased a wraparound infant carrier lined with fake sheepskin. Mooshie took to the apparatus like a joey to its mother's pouch. Tucked inside, he made himself comfy and immediately fell asleep.

With the kitten secured next to my heart, I finished the household chores and headed out for groceries. I'd forgotten about the soft carrier and its slumbering passenger when the mother of one of Simon's friends spied me in the produce section.

"Oh my gawd, I can't believe it!" she squealed, hands fluttering above the carrier. "You have a new baby! I had no idea you were even pregnant!"

"Oh no, you see yesterday we—"

"Boy or a girl?"

I could feel the "baby" stirring in his pouch. "A male, but it's not what you think. He's—"

"Simon must be thrilled to have a baby brother! What's his name?"

I hesitated. "Mooshie."

"Moshe!" she tittered, again with the flutter hands. "I love Hebrew names! How old—"

Mooshie popped out over the top of the carrier and snagged one of the woman's fingers. My enthusiastic friend stepped back, her mouth forming a perfect O. After the initial shock, she just *had* to hold him.

Once the cat was out of the bag, so to speak, Mooshie drew a crowd. Being held and mauled by a swarm of clucking, cooing shoppers agreed with him. By the time he'd been passed around the group several times, his rumbling purr could be heard in the next aisle over.

I was in awe. Unlike other cats that bolted at the first sniff of unfamiliar humans, this one was keen on being pawed at by a gaggle of adoring strangers.

Back in the car, Mooshie crawled from the depths of his pouch. Studying his face, I pressed his ears down so they were sticking out from the sides of his head—he was the spitting image of what Yoda would have looked like as a baby. He gazed up at me with those yellow bug-eyes, placed both paws on my chin, and pressed his nose to my lips.

The wee ball of fur had so fully captured my heart, I was almost giddy. "It's official now, pal. By this time tomorrow everyone in town will be talking about Moshe, the friendly Jewish kitten. They'll be lining up to manhandle you."

To signal his enthusiasm over this prospect of concentrated attention, Mooshie voiced a soft *brrrpt* sound that was halfway between a chirp and a purr.

*

I called Betty the Breeder a few days later to tell her we'd named the kitten Mushu Pork. She asked if that was with or without pancakes and I jokingly told her "with."

Mooshie's official registration papers were delivered a month later. I slid the formal document from the envelope and laughed.

Runt Boy's official registered name was Mushu Pork With Pancakes.

· 2 ·

THE KITTEN SUICIDES

"I'm a cat. We aren't required to make sense."
— Seanan McGuire, *A Local Habitation*

I am a natural-born worrier. When still a child, I developed a method to stave off the harmful effects of worrying by learning to plan ahead. Thus, the all-purpose motto I live by is, "Life is short—always be prepared."

As soon as I came up with the idea of adopting a kitten, I requested vacation time so I could devote my full attention to our new charge. This turned out to be a good thing seeing how Mooshie needed more attention than any cat I'd ever known—a condition that would last for the whole of his life.

From the beginning, it was obvious that Mooshie lived outside the boundaries of the conventional everyday cats I was familiar with. I was thus horrified to discover that my new cat was—and I doubt this diagnosis has ever been used in reference to a cat—suicidal.

The infamous *They* did a study that supposedly proved spinster cat ladies are more likely to commit suicide than catless spinsters. But what if the cat lady's *cat* is suicidal?

Hazarding a guess as to what led to this alarming anomaly in my cat's behavior, I'd say that owing to his hypersensitive nature, Mooshie was profoundly depressed over being taken away from his birth home. It didn't matter that he'd been poorly treated there—I'd seen similar depressive behavior in children who had been removed from abusive situations and placed into loving foster homes.

The depth of my cat's depression was revealed on his fifth day in residence.

After bathing him to eradicate the fleas, I toweled him off and placed him on a soft bed of flannel blankets in front of the fireplace. Mooshie studied the flames, making no attempt to shake off any excess water or lick his fur. He was so still and his gaze so fixed, I thought he was feeling relaxed and content. (It should be noted here that at the time, I was thinking in terms of how a *normal* cat would react.) It wasn't until he walked directly into the flames that I realized how wrong I was. Sure, the breeder warned us that Burmese tend to gravitate to heat no matter the source, but this was pushing the envelope.

I reached into the flames that were licking at the tips of his whiskers and pulled him out. Brushing off the singed fur on his chest, I was fully aware that had he not been wet, he would have gone up in flames like a dry Christmas tree. Miraculously, his paw pads, nose, and eyes escaped damage, which is more than I can say for the sleeves of my sweatshirt.

He was so unruffled by the whole event, (I might be anthropomorphizing here) it appeared he was disappointed at having been saved. Mindful of his melancholic mood, I searched for ways to perk him up. In my dog-eared copy of *How to Care for Your New Kitten*, the experts extolled the psychological and physical health benefits of allowing a kitten to explore a small outdoor area under supervision.

Our three-bedroom cottage was built in the late 1800s from the teak of scrapped ships that came into the San Francisco Bay to die. This and the other seven cottages on our half-acre had once provided a sunny oasis for wealthy San Franciscans who wished to escape the chilling fog that blanketed the city every summer.

The eight cottages, all painted the same dusty pink, were arranged four to a row on each side of a narrow path. It was this configuration that gave rise to our small community being called the Left and Right Bank Cottages.

Each cottage came with a mini garden plot, one or more fruit trees, exotic flowers, berry bushes, and a five-by-eight rectangle of grass. Three sides of the compound were surrounded by a wooden fence that sagged under the passionflower vines that covered them. At the front of the property, a sizable parking lot and two contemporary residential buildings shielded our lush retro-sanctuary from the busy street.

From the way Mooshie stared longingly at the grounds that ran between the two rows of cottages, I took the kitten experts at their word. Looking back on it now, I can say with some degree of certainty that Mooshie was not even remotely interested in anything the natural surroundings had to offer, other than finding a place to kill himself.

Unaware of this at the time, I outfitted my cat with a scaled-down harness attached to a ten-foot leash. I was sure that not only would the apparatus prevent Mooshie from wandering very far, it would give him a sense of security while he explored his new surroundings. Taking him into the garden alongside the cottage, I secured his leash to the base of our plum tree and retreated to my office.

My office windows conveniently looked out on the gardens, so I couldn't help but notice the strange way Mooshie circled the plum tree, studying it with all the concentration of a structural engineer calculating its measurements. Even when Jaspurr, a placid Left Bank Siamese, came by to welcome him to the home turf, Mooshie didn't even bother to acknowledge his presence with a hiss.

When he tired of examining the tree, Mooshie set about making his unorthodox potty hole preparations at its base. He spent at least five minutes digging the first hole, then spent another five minutes studying it from several angles. Dissatisfied, he dug a second hole, circled it, and squatted a few times as if trying it on for size. He went on to dig a third hole, and then a fourth. It wasn't until the seventh hole that he relieved himself, and even then he spent an inordinate amount of time covering it up, sniffing, circling, covering, and sniffing some more.

Satisfied with the results of his efforts, he shimmied up

the tree to a branch about eight feet off the ground, glanced down, and without further ado, jumped off. His leash pulled over the branch and he dangled by the neck like a furry overripe fruit. I waited for a second, sure that he'd try to right himself, or at least squirm out of the harness as any normal cat would. (Again, I'd like to emphasize that the operative word here is *normal*).

When he made no effort to help himself, I yelled for Simon and ran to the side yard. I released the harness and eased my cat's limp body to the ground, my ear to his chest. I couldn't tell if he was breathing or not, so I attempted a vigorous rubdown. When that failed to revive him, I performed kitty CPR with one-finger chest compressions and mouth-to-muzzle respirations.

Reluctant to let his pseudo sibling go so soon, Simon shouted that he was going to try something he'd seen in a Bruce Lee movie. Before I could protest, he grabbed Mooshie around the middle and swung him in a circle. Mooshie instantly snapped back to the land of the living, pulled out of Simon's hands, and bit through his jeans.

We watched in awe as the kitten jumped off Simon's leg, scampered up the plum tree, leaped to the ground, and disappeared under a hedge of olallieberries.

Through the thick tangle of thorny branches, I could see him lying on his side, calmly washing his face. It was the first grooming I'd seen him do. Jaspurr sat close by while I pleaded with Mooshie to please come out. Fifteen minutes of unproductive coaxing later, I laid back on the grass and groaned.

The Siamese cocked his head as he studied his new neighbor. I interpreted his puzzled expression as, *What's wrong with the little weirdo?*

"He's depressed," I said. "See if you can get him out of there, would you?"

Jaspurr crawled in partway, making a happy come-play-with-me call of three sliding tones—D, F, and F *ottava alta*. Mooshie repeated the call and sidled closer to the older cat until their noses touched. In a show of friendly submission, Jaspurr rolled onto his back and displayed his belly. Mooshie took this as an invitation of another sort and lost no time in burying his nose in the Siamese's belly fur, suckling anything that even remotely resembled a teat.

Jaspurr tolerated this transgression for a few seconds before he soundly thumped Mooshie's head with his back paws, then sprang to his feet and fixed my cat with a one-eyed squint. He so closely resembled John Wayne in *The Shootist,* I imagined the actor's voice coming from Jaspurr's mouth—*I won't be wronged. I won't be insulted. I won't be laid a hand on. I don't do these things to other cats, and I require the same from them.*

*

Two days before I was to return to work, my apprehension about leaving Mooshie alone for ten hours exceeded the anguish I felt the first time I left Simon with a babysitter. Before my very eyes, the cottage became a cornucopia of potentially lethal objects. I set to the task of baby-proofing (or rather, suicidal cat-proofing) our cottage. Locks were installed on the cleaning products cabinet; all string, thread, rubber bands, and sewing needles were sealed up in plastic boxes; hair hardware such as clips, and bobby pins were put into a covered bowl, and electrical cords were unplugged and pulled out of biting range.

I was installing a latch on the medicine cabinet when Jaspurr appeared and head-butted my leg. His grumbling meows made me think that a wharf rat might be in the house, or that Perch And Twirl had escaped his cage. I stepped into the hallway expecting to see either my canary or a rat, or perhaps, a rat with the canary in his mouth. The horrifying sight that met my eyes instead, was Mooshie hanging by his neck from the screen door safety chain.

Once again catapulted into emergency room nurse mode, I removed my limp kitten from the chain and, as in any pediatric emergency, began mouth-to-muzzle respirations.

Simon may have had his Bruce Lee movies to draw from, but I had my cache of nurse training films. Two seconds into my kitty CPR, the rusty vault of my memory squeaked open on a training film that featured various resuscitation methods used in the 1800s. One in particular stuck in my memory.

I rushed to the bathtub and doused my cat with cold water from the tap. Mooshie spasmodically jerked, gagged, opened his eyes, and tried to bite through my thumb. Luckily for me, my many years of hitting typewriter space bars had provided me with robust and agile thumbs, thus sparing the digit from mutilation by milk teeth.

Having again saved another of my cat's nine lives, I tucked Mooshie under warm blankets, hand-fed him tender bits of chicken liver, then petted and cooed him to sleep. It was with a sense of triumph that I returned to installing the medicine cabinet lock. Two minutes later, the jingling of the screen door safety chain reached my ears. Stepping into the hallway, I observed my cat as he crawled up the screen, fit his head inside the chain loop, and dropped.

I was dumbstruck. Was it even possible for cats to be into autoerotic asphyxiation? I rescued him again and, after thinking it over, decided to call Dr. Petrie, a local vet whose ads claimed he also specialized in animal behavior problems.

Promising myself I'd refrain from referring to the vet as Dr. PetMe, I dialed the office number. The vet tech who answered asked what the problem was. Unprepared for such a direct question, I was suddenly self-conscious. I often fielded the wildly outlandish calls that routinely came into our emergency department, so I knew there was a good chance the tech would think I was a crackpot.

I closed my eyes. "Well, I have a new kitten that seems to be, um, suicidal?"

The silence at the other end of the line spoke volumes.

I rushed on. "I know this sounds crazy, but he tried to incinerate himself and now he's purposely trying to hang himself. I'm afraid he'll—"

"Let me get this straight," the assistant said, her voice tight. "Your kitten tried to kill itself?"

At once I regretted my decision to tell anyone about my

suicidal kitten. I paused and then added sheepishly, "Yes. And I have witnesses."

"You. Have. Witnesses?" she repeated in the same stilted cadence as one of Bob Newhart's telephone routines. I thought I heard someone snicker in the background.

Unable to help myself, I let escape a snort of laughter.

"Is this a joke?" the girl asked, a hopeful lilt to her voice.

"I'm afraid not," I sighed. "But I think it would be better if I spoke directly to Dr. Petrie."

While on hold, I tried not to imagine the scene going on in the veterinarian's office. I hoped that no one I knew was sitting in the waiting room listening to the hilarity about the lunatic claiming to have a suicidal kitten.

To his credit, Dr. Petrie did not guffaw or give any indication that he thought I was insane.

"Is the animal eating and drinking?" he asked.

"Like a horse, but—"

"Moving his bowels and urinating within normal limits?"

"Beyond normal limits, but—"

"Active when he's awake?"

"Yes, but—"

"Then don't worry about it. It's probably some variation of feline separation anxiety. He'll be fine. He is a cat, Ms. Heron, not a psych patient."

There came a loud crash from the kitchen. The image of my cat pinned under the knife block flashed before my eyes. Quickly thanking the man, I hung up and was on my feet and running, already calculating how to staunch the flow of blood with a dishtowel.

Rather than bloody carnage, I found Mooshie standing paw-deep in a spreading puddle of honey. My new kitten—always on the lookout for food—had climbed onto the table, and, mistaking the five-pound can of honey for a giant tin of cat food, managed to push it off onto the floor.

Mooshie took a step, shaking one hind leg and then the other—rather like a participant in a Conga line.

I pulled him from the sticky mess by the scruff of his neck. He automatically tucked up his hindquarters as all kittens do when carried by their mothers. Looking happier than I'd ever seen him, he began to purr.

Some cats knead blankets for comfort, some suckle knobby sweaters—Mooshie wanted to be carried around by the scruff of his neck. Obviously he'd never read the list of *Things You Should Never Do to a Cat* that was in every cat advice book in the world.

From that day forward, if Mooshie was depressed or feeling insecure, I would take him by the scruff and carry him around until he purred himself to sleep.

Thus the kitten suicides came to an end and my cat was free to turn into the one-of-a-kind experience he was destined to be.

·3·

THE CAT SAVANT AND MR. GLASSMAN

*"It always gives me a shiver when I see a cat
seeing what I can't see."*
— Eleanor Farjeon *(1881 - 1965)*

ooshie's and my first year together was a time
of growth for us as individuals and as an
interspecies couple. Whenever I was asked why
I wasn't married, I'd automatically blurt out, "I have a cat,"
as if this were explanation enough. Though my inquisitors
were puzzled by my answer, it made perfect sense to me.

We had much in common—we were both products of
dysfunctional families, and the odd man out among our
siblings. While I regularly beat the pillows on my therapist's
couch in an effort to cast out the leftover demons from my
dysfunctional family of origin, Mooshie was developing his
own unique style and refining his many talents. From a
suicidal, insecure runt, he'd grown into a self-assured and
adventurous character with multiple personalities and moods.

The scruffy mat of fur he was wearing when he left the breeder's detention center had been replaced by a silky sable coat, and his once skeletal body was now a compact powerhouse of muscle. He was by far the most handsome of any cat I'd known personally. When resting, he always posed with one front paw elegantly crossed over the other, and when walking, he moved with majesty and grace.

His first collar was neon green and orange plaid. Fitted with a bright red tag, it was a bit Siegfried and Roy, but it showed off his fur. From the way he'd strut around the house each time he wore the thing, it was clear he knew how handsome he was. Mooshie was loaded with attitude. If my cat had opposable thumbs and knew how to type, I think he would have written a self-improvement book entitled, *Cattitude: How to Get It . . . and Keep it!*

His ability to fluidly slip in and out of his various personalities—Mahatma Gandhi, Harry Houdini, Einstein, Mel Brooks, and Vlad the Impaler—often left us awestruck and, at times, unnerved, especially since it was clear he had a stronger personality than I did.

I'm no ethologist, but Mooshie exhibited the ability to reason; he thought logically and then acted accordingly. Furthermore, he was empathic and quite possibly telepathic. If someone was in emotional turmoil, ill, or injured, he'd sense their distress and sit quietly nearby for as long as one needed his healing presence. Whenever bandages, casts, sprains, or infections were involved, he was fiercely protective, growling if anyone got too near the injured area.

He was the only cat I knew who could stare directly into a human's eyes and not be the first to look away. Upon meeting a new human for the first time, he'd size them up, and put that information through his human-analyzer. Ninety-nine percent of the time he accurately intuited what sort of individual they were and what they needed. The only human to ever leave him flummoxed was none other than comedian Robin Williams.

Acting as my self-appointed socialization coach, my friend Catherine took me to San Francisco one evening to see Robin Williams perform. What she didn't tell me was that she and Robin had been college sweethearts and were still very close.

It was a strange evening to be sure. One minute I was in the audience applauding the comedian, and the next, Robin was in my living room where, for four hours, he performed a brilliant improvisational comedy routine at warp speed while Catherine and I howled with laughter.

Bewildered by the highly energetic human in the bright Hawaiian shirt, Mooshie perched atop the bookcase to watch the performer bounce about the room. Ears twitching, my cat's head bobbed up and down and back and forth in his efforts to track Robin's wild antics. He probably thought the comedian was a dangerous wind-up toy whose spring was too tightly wound, for during a particularly animated routine in which Robin impersonated a psychotic talking chicken, Mooshie's fur went up and his pupils fully dilated. His human analyzer on overload, my cat slithered down the side of the bookcase and disappeared under the window seat where he hid until Robin left the following morning.

Mooshie's own wacky sense of comedic timing was spot on. He enjoyed finding various objects then carrying them around in his mouth like trophies, or presenting them to visitors as gag gifts—a way of showing he was a capable provider contributing to the community. Used band-aids, soiled undergarments, and other more embarrassing personal items would be presented to visitors such as the FedEx guy the minute they stepped into the house. (*And for you Mr. Delivery Man, I lay at your feet this fossilized condom!*)

Mooshie was fond of following me around the house like a dog, observing every move I made. His quiet contemplation of my daily habits was disconcerting, especially when he copied human behaviors and attitudes. He frequently propped himself up in a sitting position on the couch—back erect, and hind legs dangling off the cushion. Placing his elbow on the armrest, he'd cock his head to the side. The sight of my cat looking like a pintsized version of Pee Wee Herman was beyond freaky.

Mooshie took every opportunity to train me on how to best serve him. One of his basic requirements was that I carry him casually draped over my left shoulder, rather like a mink stole. I could write, cook, and clean the house, all while he hung there enjoying the scenery and waiting to see where I would take him next. Sometimes I'd catch a sideways glimpse of him while he was riding his human beast of burden—I swear I'd seen the same expression on maharajas while riding their royal elephants.

It felt good to come home from work and be greeted at the door with Mooshie's chirps of welcome. Wearing an expression of infinite compassion, he'd snap at the fizz in my club soda while I described the particularly heinous medical dramas that occurred during my shift. When I transitioned into ranting about the injustices committed against the nurses and patients because of the hospital's rapacious bean counters, he'd press his nose against my lips to shut me up. He would then dutifully follow me into the bathroom and sit on the sink while I washed my face and continued complaining about the stresses of my job.

I'd fall into bed still going on about the atrocities of life, death, and nursing politics. Mooshie would snuggle in next to me and wait until I was done complaining. He'd then meow and chirp with a slightly bored inflection which I interpreted as: *I love you, my faithful servant, but how much longer must I listen to these constant laments and denunciations?*

It might not have been the ideal relationship for a thirtysomething woman, but while I was trying to figure out where I was headed, it sure worked for me.

*

To jettison some of the angst I was feeling about my profession, that winter I began a writing project that would, in time, become my first book. Owing to the fact that I work best when I'm warm and in seclusion, I would put a nylon car cover over the Chevy and then climb inside with Mooshie. In this heated and secret hideaway, I spent many long hours writing uninterrupted while my cat slept contentedly on my lap.

Within three months, my hands began cramping from the hours of writing longhand and then typing up what I'd written on my old Remington typewriter. To remedy the situation, I took a giant leap into the Twentieth Century and purchased a new device that was just beginning to creep into the awareness of the American public—a home computer.

My first computer was a twenty-six-pound "portable" word processor the size of a suitcase. It featured a nine-inch phosphor screen and a detachable keyboard. In the first few days after the computer's arrival, Mooshie sat in my lap scrutinizing my fingers as they flew over the keyboard. With scientific detachment, he also observed my screaming, foot-stomping temper tantrums when the computer would, without warning or reason, "disappear" my work in the same manner my washing machine caused individual socks to vanish.

A fellow heat junkie, Mooshie claimed the warm top of the computer's metal case as his roost, which was exactly at my eye level. When he wasn't napping, he'd sit and stare at me while I worked. My concentration suffered at first, but I soon learned to block him out.

At the completion of each chapter, I would read it aloud in a proper British accent, playing the part of each character as I acted out the scenes. Mooshie enjoyed these forays into live theater. Ears twitching, he'd sit up, paying close attention to every word.

When I finished reading I'd ask, "Well? What do you think?" and my brilliant four-legged critic would dutifully reply, *brrrpt!* But if I read a passage that did not resonate with him, he'd take on a doleful expression, lower his head onto his front paws, and fall asleep.

Since the keyboard was the home of all function commands, a carelessly placed finger or paw could irretrievably erase hours of work in half a nanosecond. Thus it was my good fortune that Mooshie's understanding of things mechanical extended to computers. He would jump over the keyboard, walk around it, sleep next to it with his paw resting on my arm, but never once did he lay so much as one claw on any keyboard I ever used.

There were other electronic devices that Mooshie learned to use to his advantage, though not always to mine. For example, I think his preoccupation with the phone and answering machine came from his jealous nature. Each time I used the phone, Mooshie, thinking I was talking to him, would sit at my feet listening attentively and then answer in meows and chirps.

That all ended the day a caller was going on ad nauseam about something in which I had little interest. On an impulse, I held the receiver to Mooshie's ear. It was then that he must have realized that when I was talking on the phone, he was not the one being addressed and—god forbid—not the object of my full attention.

From then on if I spent more than five minutes on the phone, he would step squarely on the switch hook button and end the call. He also had the uncanny ability to detect the crucial moment in a conversation in which to disconnect for maximum impact.

For example:

"Hello, Ms. Heron? This is Dr. Strathairn's office. We've received your test results from pathology and I'm sorry to inform you that you have—"

Click!

Or, ". . . and according to your Uncle Emile's will, he left you all of his—"

Click!

As Mooshie became more proficient in matters of the phone, he taught himself how to turn off the answering machine. He was particularly sensitive to certain voices. If he liked the voice and tone of the caller, he would let the message go through; if not, he'd carefully step on the off button. My voice was one of those he did not like.

The breeder's warning that Burmese hated being left alone still haunted me, so if I got the chance I'd call Mooshie in the middle of my shift to let him know I was thinking about him. Sometimes I'd get home to find the answering machine turned off and the last message sounding like this:

"Hi, Mooshie kooshi Buddha boy. This is your mommy. Mommy woves you, you wittle snuggie wuggie—"

Click!

This proved what I have always believed—my cat not only understood what was being said, but he also held definite opinions about what was acceptable and what was useless twaddle.

After he discovered how to work the Record Memo button, I would sometimes come home to find my message tape filled to the end with sounds of deep, contented purring and an occasional *merrrow!*

Once he achieved proficiency with the Stop and Memo buttons, he went on to master the Play All Messages and Volume buttons. These he used only when his appetite was at its peak—usually between two and three a.m., the hour of my deepest sleep.

Should his kibble bowl be empty at that time, he'd first try to wake me by draping himself over my nose and mouth. If the smothering trick didn't work, he'd bite the end of my nose. When that failed, he'd open his mouth directly under my nose and exhale. In the event his cat food breath still didn't send me catapulting out of bed, he'd resort to playing old phone messages at full volume. That always worked.

It was during his telephone mastering phase that I discovered Mooshie had a drinking problem. To better understand how I stumbled upon this knowledge, I first need to explain about Mr. Glassman, our cottage poltergeist.

*

The instant I stepped into our Left Bank cottage for the first time in 1973, I sensed it was already occupied. In short order, our invisible housemate showed himself to be a feisty poltergeist who inhabited the front guest room, which also doubled as my office.

Every houseguest who spent a night in that room complained of sudden unexplained drops in temperature and the feeling that there was another presence in the room with them.

On his first (and last) visit to our Left Bank cottage, a friend of mine with a reputation for being a hard-nosed San Francisco Task Force cop, got three feet inside the front hall, froze, went pale, then backed out of the house insisting I find an exorcist posthaste.

Poltergeists have a proclivity for destructive and disturbing mischief, including loud noises, pinching, knocking, moving things about, et cetera. Our poltergeist specialized in breaking glass. Over the many years we lived in the cottage, our windows would suddenly crack without reason, and our glass-front cabinets and glass-framed prints would inexplicably shatter—to say nothing of the innumerable drinking glasses that flew out of our hands and off the shelves.

I took my friend's advice and arranged for a Catholic priest to come in and do what he could. When the blessing and prayers failed, I asked a Karuk tribal elder to conduct a smudging ceremony—a cleansing smoke bath using sacred herbs—to purify the cottage.

Nothing worked to send Mr. Glassman back to whatever spiritual jurisdiction he belonged, so we learned to live with him. We also became experts at dodging flying glass and replacing broken windows.

It was during one of Mr. Glassman's most destructive periods that one of the kitchen cabinet doors was frequently found open, with the bottle of dry cooking sherry I kept inside knocked to the floor. It seemed only logical to assume it was Mr. Glassman doing his thing.

One night I came home from work to find Mooshie spread-eagled on the kitchen floor, looking like a miniature bearskin rug. A puddle of dry sherry surrounded him like a moat. I picked him up off the floor. Head wobbling like a bobble-head doll, he let out a slurred meow, gagged, and was sick down the front of my scrub top.

Despite the sticky paw prints circling the spilled sherry, I blamed Mr. Glassman; Mooshie was simply a curious bystander who'd made the most of a bad situation.

It never entered my mind that my cat might have an alcohol problem until the night I was settled at the kitchen table rewriting a chapter. From the corner of my eye, I noticed Mooshie furtively, but steadily, advancing on the cooking sherry cabinet. He paused only long enough to give me a casual glance, as if to say in a British accent, *Oh there you are darling. I'm having a cocktail; would you like one?*

Deft as a bartender, he pushed down the cabinet door handle, stuck his paw behind the sherry bottle, and pulled it off the shelf. The stopper conveniently dislodged when it fell. Eyes half-closed, he dipped his paw into the puddle and settled in for some serious imbibing.

I scooped him up and put him on my bed. Gathering my cleaning supplies, I returned to the kitchen to find my cat again at the booze. The second he sensed my intention to cut him off, he licked faster. I pulled him away and explained that alcohol was toxic to animals. Chastened, he wobbled to my bedroom where he tried (unsuccessfully) to jump up onto the bed. He fell asleep where he landed, his raspy snores audible at the other end of the house.

I put a lock on the cabinet. But as is true for most addictive personalities, Mooshie replaced his sherry addiction with another addiction.

It was during a Left and Right Bank party that one of his adoring Right Bank fans introduced Mooshie to his first fateful potato chip. Several hours after the party broke up, I awoke to the sounds of crinkling and crunching coming from under my bed. The flashlight beam caught him inside an economy-sized bag, eating chips as if they were his sole reason for living. He paused only long enough to issue a warning growl that translated as, *Move away from the chips!*

No chip was safe in my house ever again. Wherever I hid them, my cat used his special potato chip-radar to find the bag, drag it like a fresh kill under a heavy piece of furniture, and feast.

*

One night toward the end of winter, I came home from work, shared a light snack with Mooshie, then settled down at the computer to write. The March rain beat against my cracked office window (Glassman's latest effort) as I paused to think of a word that best fit the sentence I was working on. My gaze automatically fell on my cat, who, having abandoned his efforts to make me go to bed by staring me down, was stretched over the top of the computer, fast asleep.

The word I'd searched for suddenly came to mind, but as I returned my attention to the screen, Mooshie's ears twitched, his head shot up, and his fur stood out like a carwash roller brush. The deep-throated growl that came out of him told me there was some story-worthy material heading our way.

My cat's eyes fixed on the hallway, pupils wide. Fluid as a shape-shifter, he slid over the side of the computer to the floor, his ears flared back like the tailfins on a 1959 Cadillac.

A shorted-out toaster smell filled the air as the temperature dropped—not enough to see my breath, had I been breathing, but enough to be noticeable.

Crouched, Mooshie crept out into the hall with me right behind him. Scenes from *The Amityville Horror* were running through my head when a sound like cracking ice echoed throughout the hallway. Reminiscent of a cartoon Halloween cat, Mooshie's back arched and he did that comical sideways tiptoe dance that cats sometimes do when frightened out of their minds.

The framed print that hung in our hallway swayed as a silvery fissure snaked across the glass. It crashed to the floor less than five inches from where my cat stood.

Mooshie issued a piercing screech and leaped into my arms. He shot me a glance that said, *And you wonder why I drink?* then shoved his head into my armpit.

Glassman had gone too far. At the top of my lungs, I called the poltergeist out, using language that would have made the most profane of truckers blush with admiration. I went on like this for quite a while until Mooshie pulled his head out from my armpit and stared at me like I was an unhinged wacko.

Later, after every splinter and shard of glass had been vacuumed up, the two of us retired to the kitchen for a snack. I wonder what a normal person would have thought, had they peered through our cracked window at four in the morning and seen a woman and her cat nose kissing while sharing a bowl of potato chips and a cup of English Breakfast tea.

· 4 ·

HARRY POPPINS
AND ABUSE AT THE HANDS OF THE FRENCH

"You know how it is with cats: they don't really have owners, they have staff."
— P. C. Cast, *Chosen*

One of the messages that Mooshie did not erase from my answering machine was from a reputable New York literary agent who'd seen the stories I'd written for *Reader's Digest*. Confident he could interest a publisher in a book about my life as a critical care nurse, he asked that I write a book proposal and send it to him with a few sample chapters. Consequently, early spring found me grappling with getting said proposal together—a task I knew almost nothing about.

At the time, I was having a hard time accepting hospital policies and politics that appeared to be more about the hospital's revenue and insurance companies' bottom line than the patients' safety and wellbeing. These changes were not only putting the patients at risk, but they were also causing moral injury to the nurses whose jobs were becoming increasingly stressful and dangerous.

These two matters, combined with the realization that Mooshie was my main confidant and closest companion, were a clear indication that I needed to have a life-affirming adventure.

At the age of seven, I made three promises to myself: I would never cut my hair until it reached the floor, I would never live in a place where temperatures went below seventy-two degrees, and, I would go to Europe.

The first two promises were long since blown, but there was still time to fulfill the third. Almost everyone I knew had been to Europe. If that wasn't enough to make me feel like I was missing out, they'd all come back with stories of fantastic adventures, fabulous food, and outrageous treatment at the hands of the French.

But for as much as I wanted to venture across the pond, there'd always been a myriad of reasons that made the trip impossible: raising Simon, lack of money, finishing college and nursing school, fear of the unknown, fear of flying over the Atlantic, and lastly, fear of the French. Now that I was older and most of these barriers were no longer relevant, I decided it was high time to experience French abuse firsthand. I'd had two years of conversational French in grade school, so at least I could let them know when I'd had enough.

Screwing up my courage, I went to a travel agency and came out with an itinerary, airline tickets, and a date with the travel agent. Thanks to Betty the Breeder's warnings about never leaving my Burmese, I then got a head start on worrying about who was going to take care of Mooshie. This proved to be more stressful than anything else I could have worried about, which in a perverse way, was good. Otherwise, I might have worked my knickers into a full-blown aviophobic twist about flying over the Atlantic.

*

Quite a few cats use the toilet, though most of them must undergo lengthy training to get them to that point. Not so with Mooshie. When still a kitten he would dutifully accompany people into the bathroom. His unwavering stare put most people off, especially my male guests who complained Mooshie's rapt attention induced urinary retention. Who could have guessed that my cat was using these ventures into voyeurism as learning experiences?

I was in my office one afternoon when I heard the toilet flush. Being the only human in the house, my first thought was that Mr. Glassman was branching out into plumbing. Upon investigation I found Mooshie facing the toilet tank, his hind legs teetering on the rim, and his rear quarters aimed over the bowl for a pee. Due to his diminutive size, keeping his balance was a struggle. Every so often one of his paws would slip and he'd inadvertently push down the flush lever.

I considered this a stellar accomplishment. Each time he used the facilities I'd praise him, then followed up with the real goods—some ground chicken breast or a few slices of raw tuna, and a saucer of English Breakfast tea.

For a toxoplasmosis-conscious medical professional, to live with a cat and be litterbox-free was a dream come true. I threw out the litter pan and bragged to anyone who would listen about the Amazing Mooshie who potty-trained himself. I also added this latest skill to his résumé as an incentive to prospective cat sitters who were squeamish about dealing with the litterbox.

Mooshie's new skill had been in place for a few weeks when I went on my first date with the travel agent. That I was going out with a man who was intelligent, physically fit, handsome, *and* gainfully employed, provided me with a shot of self-confidence I sorely needed.

I was a bit concerned when I learned that he'd been a psychiatrist, but left the profession because he found the travel business more challenging. However, any reservations I may have had about him were forgotten when Mr. Travel insisted we bring Simon along with us to the movies. Finding a man who didn't have issues about package deals was okay by me.

I don't recall what movie we watched, but I vaguely remember we were having a lovely time, right up until we got back to the cottage and things took an unexpected left turn into the proverbial dark alley.

After Simon went to bed, Mr. Travel and I settled in by the fireplace for an in-depth getting-to-know-you chat. We were in the middle of a riveting discussion about childhood traumas when my date asked to use the bathroom.

While he used the facilities, I went in search of Mooshie.

I'd been around enough cats to know they were the ultimate test in the consideration of a potential mate. If my cat liked the guy, I'd pursue the relationship. If the man didn't like Mooshie or vice versa, I'd nix the dude before he could say, "Get that fleabag off my face."

I was searching the upper shelves of the linen closet for my cat when I heard a series of bloodcurdling screams, followed by splashing and Mooshie's distress calls. I rushed down the hall, and without pausing to knock, stormed into the bathroom. It took a few seconds for the scene before me to fully register.

Picture this if you will: my date flattened against the wall screaming like a little girl and, emerging out of the toilet bowl like the creature from the Black Lagoon was my cat struggling to get a claw-hold on the porcelain rim.

It wasn't hard to construct the sequence of events—Mooshie had been using the toilet and slipped off the rim into the bowl. In his attempts to get a claw-hold on something, he'd inadvertently pulled the lid down on top of himself.

When my unsuspecting date lifted the toilet lid and seat together, the sight of a dripping, turd-brown furry thing with sharp teeth and huge yellow bug-eyes coming at him, had triggered his screams.

Ignoring the man pressed into the corner, I grabbed a towel and pulled Mooshie out of the toilet. I rubbed him down in front of the fireplace, then hand-fed him some finely-chopped chicken hearts.

I don't know when my date left, or what his thoughts

were about my cat or me because I never heard from him again. That was fine by me—any man who could not go with the flow in our household, was better off with someone who wasn't owned by a genius cat.

And really, who wanted a man who screamed like a little girl at the slightest provocation?

Mooshie never used the toilet again, and who could blame him? Still, I think he missed it. Every once in a while, he would jump onto the lid and push the flush lever down. With a faraway look in his eyes, he'd listen to the sound of the gurgling flush, jumping down only when the tank was finished refilling.

*

Writers are never satisfied with their work, which is why there are editors who will tell them when to stop reworking. I didn't have an editor, so I kept going back over my proposal and sample chapters every day, making changes, and then obsessing over whether I should change them back to the original.

Sensing that I was preoccupied with something other than him, Mooshie began inventing new and annoying ways to divert my attention back to where it belonged. I believe it was at this point in his life that he developed the Vlad the Impaler side of his personality and installed it with a Monty Python sense of humor.

Mooshie's preferred method of getting the notice he felt was his due involved springing out of dark corners and nipping at the feet and ankles of unsuspecting passersby. If one was foolish enough to go barefoot during what we called "Mushu Fangtooth's Oral Adventures Era," the tender area on the top of the foot was his preferred target.

I was so was engrossed in the fourth rewrite of my proposal that one evening I forgot about the Vlad the Impaler/Mushu Fangtooth menace and walked barefoot to my printer. Waiting for just such an opportunity, Mooshie attacked from behind the office door. Mouth open, teeth bared, forelegs spread wide, he jumped into the air and came down snaggletooth-first on top of my right foot.

Cursing, laughing, hopping, and running simultaneously, I lunged for him as he bobbed and weaved around the furniture, his eyes wide with glee. I lost sight of him and was tiptoeing past my bedroom when he leaped from behind the door, his mini-claws grabbing onto my Achilles tendon—the same tendon I'd severed at age eleven in a freak gardening accident involving a razor-sharp spear head spade. It was also the same tendon that was still sensitive as blazes to the touch.

I yelped in pain and fell onto the bed clutching my ankle. Mooshie froze in place then jumped up and put his paw on my arm. I took this for a sincere apology—he certainly *looked* sorry—but as I reached over to give him a reconciliatory rub behind the ears, he nipped my arm and jumped off the bed, ready for another round of chase and bite. I got a pinch hold on the scruff of his neck and brought him up short, only slightly offended by his contented purring as he swiveled his head one side to the other, straining to bite me again.

I pushed him into the bathroom and closed the door. "You need to chill out, buddy."

There were a few insincere meows of repentance and then nothing. I made up my mind to let him stew. Ten minutes passed without so much as a chirp from the other side of the door. I knew from experience that when a child is quiet for too long, trouble is afoot.

I tried the door and found it locked; a circumstance I found baffling. All the doors in the Left and Right Bank cottages were the 1880s originals. Made of solid wood, the doors were equipped with vintage ornate metal locks that had a sliding button on the upper edge. At some point, Mooshie must have taken note of how we locked the door and filed the procedure away for future use.

I reminded myself that this was an animal who, without the benefit of opposable thumbs, had mastered the art of opening a variety of doors. I'd watched in wonder as he pulled down or pushed up door levers, disengaged hook and eye latches, or held doorknobs between his forelegs and twisted them until the latch bolt released. Sliding a small button was no challenge.

Thinking I'd get in through the bathroom window, which was *always* unlocked, I went around to the side of the house and set up the ladder.

"Here I come, buddy boy," I yelled, and pushed on the window . . . which was locked. How Mooshie had mastered *that* trick was anybody's guess.

Through a gap in the curtains, I could see my cat playing his favorite game of batting a tinfoil ball around the inside of the bathtub. Tiring of that game, he then engaged in the sport of sliding down the tub's backrest.

I was tapping on the glass to get his attention when Joni, Jaspurr's Left Bank human, approached. "Spying on someone using the facilities? I would have thought you'd have your fill of that sort of thing, working in the hospital."

"It's Mooshie. He's locked himself in the bathroom. I was giving him a time-out and he must have pushed the lock button."

Joni looked skeptical. "I've watched him open doors, but locking them seems tricky for a cat, even one like Mooshie. You aren't thinking of breaking the window, are you? I mean, you don't want to encourage Mr. Glassman."

"No, but I *am* thinking of taking the door off the hinges."

It was a brilliant idea without a future, given that the hinges were buried under innumerable coats of paint. I tried paint remover, WD-40, and hammering the pivot pins out of the knuckles, before I came to the realization nothing was going to budge them.

Joni pulled in a couple of neighbors from the Right Bank to look at the door. Shortly thereafter Simon came home from school with two of his friends. As a group, we examined, pulled, and prodded the stubborn door until we all came to the same solution—call the landlord.

Lindo the landlord, was a sweet older gentleman of Italian descent who, though he wasn't thrilled about Mooshie being added to our household, understood the practicality of having a cat around to keep down the rat population.

Twenty minutes later, he entered the cottage, lugging a bucket of tools.

Crowded into the narrow hallway, the eight of us brainstormed until it was determined that Lindo would have to remove the hinge plate screws and pull the door off. When that idea failed, he grudgingly chiseled the hinges out of the doorframe. The whole time my landlord labored, I could hear Mooshie's tinfoil ball skittering around the tub.

The door was loosened, and, after a short burst of applause, removed.

Mooshie was curled up in the sink, one of his forelegs draped over the side. Like a celebrity meeting his adoring public, he yawned and stretched.

Encouraged by our chorus of delighted ooohs and ahhhs, he stood and sang a series of chirpy meows. My cat must have sensed Lindo's initial ambivalence about his tenancy given that he pawed at the man's overalls, begging to be held.

Enchanted by the purring animal licking his face, Lindo sang a little tune in Italian and carried Mooshie out of the bathroom with the same gentleness one might employ with a slumbering newborn.

Before he left, Lindo stopped cooing long enough to say that I could call on him anytime "Mushy" needed a helping hand.

Regrettably, that time came two days later when, in a fit of pique over my extended absence due to my working a double shift, Mooshie again locked himself in the bathroom. Somewhat less enamored with a cat that promised to routinely increase his workload, Lindo lectured "Mushy" at length and disassembled the lock once and for all.

*

Mooshie had his quirks. So, lest I give the false impression that he was the Ken Jennings of the feline set, there were times my cat behaved more like a doofus than any kind of feline Einstein. Auto-asphyxiation using a screen door chain aside, Mooshie had an uncanny habit of allowing his tongue to hang out of his mouth whenever he was relaxed. I would sometimes find him staring off into space, his tongue lolling, and blobs of saliva pooling at the corners of his mouth. He seemed to enjoy getting his snaggletooth stuck in things like small sticks or art gum erasers and then carrying on with his day as if they weren't there.

On the other hand, I have to admit he *did* teach me many valuable life lessons. Take, for instance, his head-banging tutorial.

My bed was flanked on one side by a window looking out on a row of trees and bushes that served as a popular hangout for neighborhood birds. Each day Mooshie would position himself on the edge of the bed, his little jaw chattering pre-attack declarations while his whisker pads quivered. As the tension mounted, foam formed at the sides of his mouth.

Thirty seconds into this behavior, he would spring as if from a catapult, headfirst into the window. He would then fall into the four-inch crack between the bed and the wall. Face up, all four paws in the air, he would sink down to the floor a few inches at a time.

Once recovered, he'd jump up on the bed and reenact this sequence five or six more times until he regained some sense of dignity and wobble away, tail between his legs. He repeated this display of pointless idiocy every day as a demonstration of poor judgment.

Six weeks before my trip to Europe, the most devastating of my ex-romances showed up at my door bearing the verbal equivalents of scentless roses. At first I was resistant, not because of any good sense that might have penetrated my thick skull during my many hours of therapy, but because Mooshie's hackles went up the second he laid eyes on the jerk.

Did I heed what my cat was trying to tell me? Alas, the lure was too great. I *had* to stick my arm into the shark's mouth one more time to make *sure* it really hurt.

One morning after the newly reinstated emotional vampire savaged my heart yet again, Mooshie performed his head-banging stunt, trying by example to make me conscious of my own foolish behavior.

As he rammed his head into the window repeatedly, the question that came to mind was how a cat who was so exceptionally bright could also be so clueless about continuing to strive for something that he *knew* was impossible to have.

Like, duh.

And that was the end of the vampire boyfriend.

*

As previously indicated, I am a planner and organizer. A month before I was to leave for Europe, my suitcase was so perfectly packed and arranged, it was an obsessive-compulsive's wet dream.

To my knowledge Mooshie had never seen a suitcase, but he immediately perceived it as a threat. He would circle the roller bag, then savagely attack it. Had he been the type of cat who sprayed, I'm sure he would have used the suitcase as his target.

My packing completed, I then arranged to take advantage of my eight-hour layover in New York to personally deliver my proposal packet to the prospective literary agent.

I then turned my full attention to finding a live-in cat nanny.

First I typed up a list of requirements the applicant would have to agree to if they were to be awarded the honor of taking care of Mooshie. The most cardinal of all the cat care commandments was that the chosen nanny had to be 100 percent dedicated to my cat's wellbeing. I wanted a person who could outsmart a cat that was adept at devising ingenious ways to escape. This required daily security surveillance for new hidey-holes and breaches in escape route barriers.

Second, my cat's nanny would have to adore Mooshie full-heartedly. Third, the chosen nanny would have to be a homebody who would spend their free time entertaining my cat. Fourth, Mooshie would have to be allowed to sleep with the nanny, even if that meant offering his or her face as a roost. Last but not least, the au pair who won the honor of caring for Mooshie would be required to follow my eight typed pages of cat nanny instructions.

I went over my pitifully short list of friends and was dismayed to realize that not one of them qualified for the job. Everyone I knew inconveniently had families, or hated cats, or were workaholics and had no time for a needy feline.

As time grew short, I was forced to ease up on the requirements. Okay, so they didn't *have* to love my cat, but they couldn't hate cats either. I adjusted the homebody requirement to a humble request that they spend at least an hour a day engaging with Mooshie. The sleeping arrangement requirement was deleted altogether since Mooshie would make it happen anyway.

In this way I was able to edit the eight pages of instructions down to five by deleting such minutia as recording the number of fleas found and killed during his daily flea combing.

I made sure Mooshie was asleep in another part of the house before making my final round of calls; I didn't want him to know I was having to do a hard sell to find a nanny. Starting with the A-B's, I called every person in my address book, even if I hadn't spoken to them in years. I begged, cajoled, and promised the moon. When those tactics failed, I began making offers of cold, hard cash.

Ten days before I was to leave, I found a neatly printed note tacked to the notice board in the nurses' lounge:

Middle-aged nursing student presently living in his car with anatomy and physiology textbooks. Will work in exchange for temporary room and board. Interacts well with children, plants, and pets.

Ask for Harry the stethoscope jockey.

I practically broke a finger in my haste to dial the number.

The stethoscope jockey showed up for his interview dressed in student nurse scrubs with the hems of his pants stuffed into cowboy boots. He was a Paul Bunyan-sized guy which meant more footage for my cat to climb. But the biggest bonus was Harry's full beard—Mooshie was entranced at once. I was thrilled to see Harry smiling as my cat foraged through his beard with an intensity that made me think there might actually be something nesting in there. This was an excellent indication that the young nursing student's level of tolerance was high.

Introductions made, the three of us sat in the living room to discuss my detailed instruction list. I began by making sure Harry understood that taking care of Mooshie would be like going to cat care boot camp.

I finished going over the instructions and was chatting on about how delicate Mooshie was when it registered that man and beast were completely ignoring me as they both slid to the floor for some rough-and-tumble play.

Harry was the answer to all my prayers—my very own male version of Mary Poppins come to save the day.

*

The day before my departure, I suffered through one of those meat grinder therapy sessions that left me reeling. From there I went directly to the ER where I spent the next nine hours tending to humanity in its rawest form. By the time I got home I was mentally, emotionally, and physically exhausted.

Sensing my distress, Mooshie would not let me out of his sight. I crawled into bed still jabbering on about how stressed I was, when my cat tentatively curled up beside me, keeping his eyes fixed on my face—as if he were afraid I might be turning rabid.

I took several deep breaths and closed my eyes, waiting for the quick slide into sleep. Instead, my brain diverged into hyper-worry mode that went something like this:

In less than twelve hours I need to be at the airport. I'm worried about being worried that I won't be able to sleep and if I don't sleep I'll be so exhausted by the time I get to New York I won't be able to find my prospective literary agent let alone have a coherent discussion with him and then he'll think I'm a wacko and not accept my proposal, and then if I can't sleep on the plane to London I'll be rendered psychotic from sleep deprivation so that by the time I hit Heathrow Airport, I'll have to be put in a sanatorium and given tea and biscuits five times a day until I die.

I'm not sure how, but somewhere amid all that worrying, I fell asleep.

At five a.m., strains of discordant, eerie music jolted me awake. Following the otherworldly tones, I found Mooshie standing on the piano bench, pawing the black and white keys. He threw me a casual look that said, *Any last requests, Dollface?*

*

I was to meet my prospective literary agent at a certain Manhattan café. It wasn't until I reached the place that it dawned on me I didn't have the foggiest idea of what he looked like. Armed only with the knowledge that he spoke with a distinguished British accent, I kept my eyes peeled for a Sir John Gielgud lookalike.

A dapper older gentleman approached with some hesitance. His impeccable three-piece suit had Sir John Gielgud written all over it, although the red patent leather shoes did give me pause.

Atwitter with nerves, I boldly stepped forward and shook the man's hand, blathering on about how wonderful it was to meet him. He seemed bewildered at first, but my enthusiasm must have done something to bolster his confidence in that he slipped his arm around my waist and tried to kiss me.

Only when he began groping my backside did I wonder if I'd given the wrong impression. Or, maybe New York literary agents expected this depth of familiarity upon meeting—breaking the ice right away, so to speak.

The man was trying to lead me away from the café when I heard my name and felt a tap on my shoulder. I turned to find a tall, slender man who looked nothing like Sir John Gielgud. Raising an eyebrow, he gave the cad at my side the hairy eyeball.

The stranger released his grip.

Somewhat abashed, I shook the agent's hand. "Thank God!" I gushed, jerking my thumb in the direction of the imposter. "The three-piece suit—it threw me. I was looking for a Sir John Gielgud look-alike."

My prospective agent grinned. "I assure you that Sir John Gielgud and I wouldn't be caught dead in red patent leather shoes."

Laughing, I brushed off the ersatz agent and my embarrassment, and entered the café. The next two hours were a blur, although I do remember looking at the menu, shocked that a cup of soup cost more than what I earned in an hour. I also distinctly recall handing over my book proposal and chapters to the agent, feeling like I was putting a much-loved child up for adoption.

What most stands out in my mind, and the thing that clinched the deal, was that we were both devoted cat lovers who belonged to outstanding felines. After swapping Burmese and Maine Coon stories, we sealed our agency contract with a good old-fashioned handshake.

As we bid each other *au revoir,* I squelched the Italian half of me that wanted to hug the man and kiss the hem of his sport jacket in gratitude. He *was* British after all, and in light of the earlier debacle outside the café, I didn't want him to think I was one of those loose California women he'd probably heard so much about. Instead, I called upon my British/Dutch side to properly thank him and promise to refrain from going off with red-shoed strangers until I heard from him again.

*

Europe was marvelous. Britain's countryside and the dry British humor had me seriously considering moving there—until I learned there was a six-month quarantine on imported cats. Also, using the United Kingdom's phone system to call the U.S. was not an easy task. First, I had to search for a call box with a phone that actually worked. Then there were the operators, some of whom sounded as though they were speaking an entirely different language. On the day I manage to get through to the cottage, the phone rang six or seven times when the operator cut in. "It would appear that no one wishes to speak to you."

Disregarding the gibe, I told her to continue to let it ring. Meanwhile, I fought off visions of my cat scared and alone, sitting on top of Harry, who lay dead, inadvertently smothered by my cat while he slept. On the twelfth ring, Harry answered out of breath.

"Why isn't the answering machine on?" I asked.

"Oh sorry, Mooshie switched it off before he left."

"If you put a plastic basin over the machine, he can't . . ." I paused. "Wait. What do you mean, before he *left*? Where did he go?"

Harry sighed. "He didn't go anywhere. I mean he's here, ah, somewhere."

I willed myself not to get excited. After all, I was in the land of stiff upper lips and tea drinkers. "Have you and Mooshie been at the dry sherry?"

"No, but I *have* been crawling around the attic among the hundreds of calcified dead rats, trying to devise a way to get your cat out of the wall."

Groaning, I rested my head against the booth's glass doors. "Explain please."

"I woke up this morning and he was gone. It was like he disappeared into thin air. Then I heard him making chirpy bird noises, so I tracked him to somewhere inside the wall between the living room and the kitchen. I've been trying to get him to come out for the last two hours. I can't believe he'd make me worry. I thought we were buddies."

"You got off easy, Harry. He's a mischievous cat with all sorts of tricks that will make your hair turn gray. Wait an hour. If he got himself in there, he'll get himself out. If not, you'll find an electric can opener in the laundry room. Use it to open a can of tuna, it might jar his memory as to where the exit is. If he doesn't come out by tomorrow, call the landlord—I'm sure he'll be thrilled about cutting through the wall."

In Milan, the Italian phone system presented me with a new set of hurdles. The lines were frequently jammed, and my Italian was limited. Ultimately I connected with an operator who, oddly enough, spoke English with a Boston accent. She suggested I try calling after midnight. I checked Harry's work schedule and thought it best if I called on his day off. On the appointed evening, to keep myself awake, I walked to the Duomo and watched inebriated tourists stumble about, desperately trying to remember the way back to their hotels.

The Boston-Italian operator had not steered me wrong. I got through to California on the first try. Harry, who was at that moment relaxing on the window seat reading a book, picked up on the first ring.

"How's my cat?" I asked.

"Out of the wall. He was standing by his bowl before the electric opener got halfway around the tuna can. Right now he's somewhere in my beard snoring."

"Put him on, would you?"

There came the rustling of clothes and then the wheezy sound of my cat's respirations. "Hey, Pumpkin! Mommy misses you. Harry tells me you've been in the wall. Please don't go in there—you might bump into a rat that's bigger than you. Do you miss your mommy?"

I held my breath until there came the unmistakable sound of purring followed by his sweet, distinctive *brrrpt!*

It was enough to hold me for the rest of the trip.

*

Despite the French, France was superb. The food was out of this world and the natural beauty of the country was breathtaking. I traveled from Paris to Giverny's Monet gardens, then on to the Loire Valley, the French Riviera, and back to the incomparable majesty of Paris.

As an American woman touring France alone in the mid-1980s, I admit the abuse was everything I'd been told to expect and more. Despite my friendly smile and elementary French, I was insulted, spit on, cursed, shunned, physically assaulted, forced into life-threatening situations, and repeatedly swindled.

By the time I left, I could not wait to get home to my cat.

· 5 ·

SINGING B-FLAT:
AN ALTERED STATE

*"There are two means of refuge from the miseries
of life: music and cats."*
— Albert Schweitzer (1875 – 1965)

U pon my return from Europe, Mooshie refused to
come to me at first. Instead, he hid behind
Harry's beard. I attempted to pull him out, but his
paw shot from the center of the beard, claws extended, like
a tame version of the chest-burster scene from *Alien*.

To show his displeasure over my month long absence,
my cat remained cool toward me for two days. Rather than
sleeping on the pillow next to mine, or nestled into the
crook of my neck, he began sleeping on Simon's pillow—a
serious infraction of the rules due to Simon's asthma. I tried
to entice him into my lap with a bite-sized piece of fresh
tuna, but he snatched the morsel out of my hand and ran

away without so much as a chirp of appreciation.

At the bottom of the prodigious stack of bills and junk mail that had accumulated during my absence, I found a formal-looking envelope from my literary agent. I opened it, expecting nothing more than an apology for not being able to interest any editors in my book, and wishing me luck on future projects.

I read the first sentence several times before the full meaning of it sank in—an editor at Atheneum wanted to publish my book.

I responded to this news by screaming and jumping around the living room like a three-year-old on a Mountain Dew high. Unused to such a primitive display from his normally staid and sober human, Mooshie came out of his hidey-hole to watch the old lady go berserk. Unable to restrain himself, he sprang into the air and nipped my naked foot as it came within biting range. I believe it was his way of letting me know I was forgiven. It was also a warning that the next time I left him, he wouldn't be so easy on me.

*

For a writer, landing a book contract is like winning the 100 million dollar lottery. Unlike winning the lottery, it does bring with it a few downsides, such as deadlines and the pressure to meet them.

I became a person driven, writing sixteen hours a day on my days off, and six hours on the days I worked at the hospital. I was focused on my writing, but not so engrossed that I missed the change taking place in Mooshie.

Up to this point, my cat had been experiencing adolescence like a normal human teenage boy, which is to say he was full of mischief and had an appetite so voracious (or vicious) that I again had him tested for worms. Mooshie was so insistent on being fed whenever he wanted, that he invented one of his most annoying tricks of all time.

His favorite food dish was a shallow stainless steel bowl. Any time he found the bowl empty, he would push down one edge and then let it fall with a loud clang. He would do this ten or so times in quick succession, producing a sound as jarring as a chuck wagon triangle dinner bell. After a week of being jerked out of a sound sleep, my initial amusement came to an end. I remedied the situation by supergluing the bowl to a rubber mat.

My intuition told me that other than his insatiable appetite, something else was going on with my cat, though I couldn't quite put my finger on what it was. He was anxious and out of sorts, as if there were some underlying torment that was eating at him.

He began following me from room to room, demanding to be held and reassured. Whenever I needed to leave the house, he'd throw himself down in front of the door and refuse to move. If I tried opening the door by pushing him inch by inch, he would sink his claws into the rubber weather strip on the bottom of the door and hold fast. If I didn't move quickly enough, he'd leap to the other side of the door and throw himself down again, voicing chirps and rumbles of complaint. From his tragic expressions, I could almost hear his pitiful entreaties: *But I need you. How can you leave me all alone?*

At a loss to figure him out, I turned up my radar and waited for my cat to make known what was going on in the mysterious world of Mushu Pork With Pancakes.

He didn't make me wait long.

It was through my love of singing that Mooshie let me in on what was bugging him. I sing everything—ballads, country, jazz, opera—you name it. (Well okay, maybe not yodeling.)

One evening as I was washing dishes and singing some self-composed aria, I hit and held a clear B-flat. Mooshie, who had been asleep on top of the stove, jerked awake, his pupils dilated. From deep in his throat came a peculiar warbling sound.

I stopped singing and his pupils returned to normal size.

He jumped down from the stove and sniffed my legs with a predatory gleam in his eyes that was miles beyond freaky. I slowly backed out of the kitchen. Mooshie followed, moving in a cross between a John Wayne swagger and a Fred Astaire shuffle.

Living dangerously, I hit another B-flat and again his pupils dilated. Without so much as a *may I please,* he climbed onto my leg, wrapped his forelegs around my calf, got a tooth-hold on my shin, and began humping like a merchant marine on leave. While he humped, he bore a startling resemblance to the devil—as in Satan, Beelzebub, and Lucifer.

I went from B-flat to a yelp. In an instant he came to his senses and ceased humping. What a revelation it was to learn that dogs are not the only species that hump humans' legs. But who would have thought *cats*? And certainly not a cat as savvy as Mooshie.

To avoid any further assaults on my leg, I took up singing in the shower, but the water proved to be no deterrent; it was the cleanest period of Mooshie's life.

The day I caught my cat eyeing both Jaspurr *and* Perch And Twirl in that same salacious manner, I realized something had to be done.

To neuter or not to neuter, that was the question. Taking a chance that he would not remember Mooshie's suicide attempts, I decided to call Dr. Petrie. I explained the whole B-flat conundrum and inquired if he knew of other cats being similarly affected when hearing certain tones.

Dr. Petrie reminded me that Mooshie was an anomaly in the feline world, and then jovially intimated that someday my cat's brain might make for a fascinating study.

"But seriously," he concluded, "Mooshie needs to be neutered, the sooner the better. He's overdue."

I called the Snip N' Go Animal Birth Control Clinic and took the first opening they had. That night as we settled into bed, I informed Mooshie he was going to have an operation. I then went on to describe in anatomical detail what was going to happen, and how much happier he was going to be once he was relieved of certain organs that would someday lead him into trouble.

Thirty seconds into my explanation, he yawned and slipped under his pillow.

A few hours later Simon shook me awake. "Mom get up, you've gotta see this. Mooshie is in the kitchen and he's—"

I opened one eye and peeked at the clock. "It's two a.m.," I groaned. "Unless you've caught him penning his memoirs, I'll look in the morning. Go back to bed."

Simon tugged at my arm. "Seriously Mom, Mooshie's acting weird."

I pulled the blanket over my head. "If he was acting normally, I'd worry—weird, not so much. Let me sleep."

"No, Mom. He's different somehow, like maybe he's lost his marbles for real this time."

I gave in with a sigh and shuffled my way to the kitchen, where my cat was crouched on the table trying to chew through the wooden handle of an old fillet knife. He glanced at his audience, wondering, no doubt, why his humans were up at such an hour.

"Watch this," Simon laughed, reaching for the knife.

Mooshie issued a warning growl, jumped to the floor with it still clamped in his jaws, and hauled it into the farthest corner of the kitchen. I'd seen him do something similar the time he dragged a four-pound roasting chicken off the kitchen table.

"What the hell has gotten into him?" I whispered, baffled and fascinated by the sight.

"Maybe he's teething," Simon said, grabbing for his pseudo-brother's tail.

Escaping Simon's grasp, Mooshie darted from the kitchen, the knife still clenched between his teeth. The last I saw was the glint of the blade as my cat shot out the back door and into the night.

I panicked. The breeder's warning that Burmese have no

survival skills was no exaggeration. The few times Mooshie contrived a way to escape, he made straight for the main street and plopped himself down in the middle of the lane. We were always able to retrieve him in time, but it was clear that shreds of his suicidal nature still lurked deep within.

"Grab a flashlight and search along the creek," I moaned. "I'll check the street and head north."

We searched for two hours, tramping through people's backyards and peering under parked cars, all without luck. I went back to bed and tried to block out images of Mooshie lost and scared, or worse, his mangled body lying in a gutter.

Focusing on the natural flow and rhythm of my breath, I was beginning to relax when the sound of my cat's asthmatic purr reached my ears. I felt a rush of relief as I lifted his pillow and found him safe and sound, curled up tight as a pill bug. He yawned and held up his forelegs, his signal that he wanted to be cuddled. I held him close, murmuring inane love pledges and praising him for returning home all on his own. Once he reached his cuddle threshold, he wriggled free and meowed for his pillow.

I was leaving for the hospital the following day when Joni came roaring into the parking lot. "Get in! I just spotted Mooshie over on Sycamore Avenue."

I cocked my head. "Um, Joni? Mooshie's on the window seat in the living room. I saw him there less than five seconds ago."

"No way! I'm telling you he's over on Sycamore Avenue. Let's go before he gets hit by a car."

"He's here," I insisted. "Come in and see for yourself."

Joni followed me to the window seat where Mooshie sat contemplating the garden. Her jaw dropped. Five minutes ago he was over on Sycamore. I chased the sucker for two blocks. I came within a foot of getting my hands on him!"

"You probably saw a black cat with yellow eyes. Without a close look, you wouldn't be able to tell the difference. I've done it myself."

"No! I'm telling you it was Mooshie. He had the same snaggletooth, the same red collar, the same silver bell, and the same red ID tag."

Not knowing what else to say, I offered my delusional neighbor a glass of lemonade and suggested she might want to see an ophthalmologist, or maybe a neurologist.

On one of our last warm and breezy days of summer, I got a head start on fall housecleaning. I blocked off the front porch and the back patio gate to keep Mooshie contained, then opened all the doors and windows to give the house a proper airing out.

As I began gathering the wash, Mooshie ran to the laundry shed. For my cat, riding the mechanical monster that bucked and rocked during every spin cycle is what a Disneyland ride is to a ten-year-old boy. Mooshie watched expectantly as I emptied the laundry into the washer.

"There's room for the front porch chair covers," I said. "Wait here while I grab them, okay?"

Mooshie chirped in reply and sat back to wait.

I walked through the house, swung open the porch screen door, and found Mooshie sitting on one of the

74

rocking chairs contentedly bathing himself.

I picked him up and set him in the sun while I stripped off the chair covers and headed back to the washing machine—where I found Mooshie patiently waiting for the ride to begin.

My brain hiccupped.

I stopped and carefully examined him. Mooshie purred in his signature asthmatic rumbling way. His snaggletooth gleamed in the sun and the tip of his tongue protruded from his mouth.

Setting him down, I strode through the house to the front porch where Mooshie sat on the rocking chair, his snaggletooth in full view.

Humming the theme song to the *Twilight Zone,* I inspected the cat on the rocker, tail to nose. Same snaggletooth, same red collar, same silver bell, and same red ID tag. Even the asthmatic rumble was the same. Then I lifted his leg and peeked.

Unless Mooshie had evolved to his truest self with gender-affirming surgery without my ever knowing, the Burmese I was holding was a female.

The screen door pushed open and the real Mooshie wound himself around my ankle. I put his doppelganger down and the two snuggled up as if they'd been together since the womb. Side by side they were identical.

I turned the female's tag over and read: *MAD ROSE.* According to the address, Mad Rose lived directly behind us on the other side of the creek. I dialed the phone number, noting with some amazement that apart from two transposed digits, it was the same as ours.

The similarities didn't stop there. When Charlotte, Mad Rose's human, came to retrieve her cat, we gaped at each other—we could easily have passed as sisters. As members of the Burmese Humans Club, we set to talking about our eccentric cats.

Though the two felines were similar in many ways, Mad Rose and Mooshie did have their differences. Mad Rose was six months older and Canadian-born, she was an outdoor cat, free to roam whenever the urge moved her and, she loved chewing on wooden utensil handles.

Charlotte confessed that Mad Rose was a skilled thief who specialized in burglarizing stranger's homes whenever she found an open door, window or pet flap. Her garage was filled with Mad Rose's booty: kitchen utensils, two winter parkas with fur collars, children's toys, hats and gloves, and the cat's most impressive score—a tennis racket.

"I thought I was losing what was left of my mind," I said as we watched the two cats play. "I wonder if they ever traded places, trying out each other's life for a day or two?"

Charlotte smiled. "I hope they had a good laugh over it if they did. By the way, do you have a teenage son who collects baseball cards and is missing a 49ers ballcap?"

I blinked. "Ah, yeah."

"Not only is he missing his ballcap, but he's also been robbed of a few of his 1981 Chicago Cubs baseball cards. Mad Rose came home about three months ago with a Leon Durham. Since then she's scored a card every couple of weeks. She brought home Jerry Morales two nights ago. I'll return them, but your son should keep them locked up."

"Aren't you worried that Rose might be stolen or hit by a car?"

Charlotte thought the question over then said, "Not really. We don't live on a busy main street and she's good about not straying too far from the house. It also helps that I had her spayed early. The vet told me it would keep her from making a break for the hills. Alas, it didn't stop her from pilfering."

I felt a pang of disappointment with the revelation that Mad Rose was not able to reproduce. Even though I was fully aware of my cat's appointment with the chopping block, the idea of mating Mad Rose and Mooshie had slipped into my mind. It was enough to make me reconsider my decision to have Mooshie neutered.

I didn't spend much time mulling over the neutering issue because the resolution to that dilemma soon came on the heels of a harmless party-prank-turned-SPCA-incident.

*

My cat was an aberration of his species. While most cats are categorized as antisocial, standoffish, and solitary creatures, Mooshie was a party animal. He thrived on adoring attention and manhandling. If he had his way, he would party seven days a week, be the first to arrive, and the last to be carried out. It didn't matter how many humans handled or fawned over him, people were Mooshie's main source of power, confidence, and entertainment.

Five days before Mooshie's appointment at Snip N' Go, the Left and Right Bank residents held a Sunday tequila and potluck brunch on the common area between our cottages. Outfitted with his fifty-foot leash, Mooshie—referred to as "The Cat on a Rope" by the other residents—was making himself available for mauling, and for any treats the humans might drop or throw his way.

Thinking it "toooo cute," one Right Bank resident who was a few tequila sunrises too many over the horizon, tied a helium smiley face balloon to Mooshie's halter while he was busy wolfing down a handful of potato chips.

After my cat had exhausted everyone's supply of snacks, he waddled off in search of some blistering hot blacktop. Halfway to the parking lot, his leash snagged on a protruding tree root. Feeling the drag on the rope, Mooshie turned to investigate.

How he perceived the bright yellow happy face hovering over him with its demented single-line smile and bottomless black eyes, can only be imagined. He let out an ear-splitting howl, jumped two feet into the air, then ran like a bat out of hell, his fur sticking out at all angles in the manner of a cartoon cat being electrocuted.

Mooshie careened up the side of the garage, bounced off, flew once around the parking lot, and slid under the Chevy. He would have run farther, but the rope caught under one of the Chevy's rear tires and pulled him up short.

The balloon exploded the instant it met the searing blacktop.

It took the better part of an hour to lure him out from

under the car, and even then it took a while before his pupils came back down to normal size.

Considering the blow to his ego, it wasn't surprising that Mooshie went missing the following morning. How he accomplished getting through the bedroom window despite it being open only three inches was beyond my comprehension. I tried to imagine my cat squishing himself through the crack in the same way rats did, but my mind balked at the vision.

I told myself that my little shape-shifter would be back of his own accord—he knew where his kibbles and raw tuna came from. By late afternoon, when he still had not returned, I dispatched Simon to scour the neighborhood while Jaspurr and I checked around the cottages. Simon returned an hour later, sans cat.

I was heading for the phone to call the SPCA lost and found hotline when the phone rang.

"Is this the owner of Mushu Pork?" The man's voice was low and businesslike.

"Thank God! Do you have him? Is he—?"

"He's fine," the man assured me. "He's been entertaining my office staff for the better part of the day. They wouldn't let me call you until they each had a chance at spoiling him."

I groaned. Honing his skills as a charmer, Mooshie had again seduced a bevy of toadying admirers into doing his biding. His innate feline sense of entitlement and superiority was already something to be dealt with—I didn't even want to imagine what he'd be like if he became the town celebrity cat.

"Where are you? I'll come around with his straitjacket and fetch him."

"You don't have far to go. We're in the Preston Graphic Design building."

I snorted. Maybe Mooshie wasn't as adventurous as I thought.

"You mean the Preston building *next door*? The one I can reach out my kitchen window and touch?"

"The very same," the man chuckled. "I'm Bob Preston, and your cat was waiting on our doorstep this morning. He ran in and jumped up on my desk the minute I opened the door. He settled in for a nap like he'd lived here all his life." He paused. "He drinks tea. Were you aware of that?"

There was an underlying tone of disapproval in his voice that made me cautious. "Why no," I lied, "I wasn't."

"Not only that," he went on, "but I'm afraid my staff fed him a couple of those small bags of potato chips and a can of tuna for lunch. He preferred the chips over the tuna. I can't say I've ever seen a cat growl over potato chips."

"Uh-huh. Good thing you didn't have any dry sherry around, or you'd never get rid of him. Well, if it's all the same to you, I'll just head on over and pick him up—unless you want to hand him to me through the kitchen window?"

The man abruptly changed tact. "Does this cat have papers?"

"Papers?" An uncomfortable sensation crept into my stomach. Perhaps Bob was some sort of SPCA undercover agent. Still, I had a serious struggle with my mouth to keep from saying, *Papers? We don't need no stinking papers!*

"Um, what papers?"

"He's a Burmese, isn't he? I assume he's registered?"

"Oh, *those* papers. Yes, he is registered."

"And from the way he's been humping my leg, I'm assuming he's still intact?"

I buried my face in my free hand, feeling simultaneously mortified and jealous, though I suppose to a horny cat, one leg was just as good as another.

"Oh. Sorry about that. I've been lax about having him neutered, but he does have an appointment this Friday at the clinic."

There was a hesitation from the other end of the line. "Would you hold off on that? Let me talk to my wife first?"

I tried to make sense of this, but my mind could not quite take the sharp left turn needed to get there. "Excuse me?"

"I own a Burmese female that went into her first heat two days ago. She's young, but your man here looks like he might be able to get the job done."

"Get the job done?" I repeated, astounded that my cat had sniffed out the owner of a Burmese female in heat, then showed up at his office to pander his services. Maybe Mooshie was even more brilliant than I thought.

Bob got right down to business. "What would you want for a stud fee?"

I snickered at the thought that I was pimping my cat. "How about if I have my choice of one of the kittens?"

Mr. Preston agreed and the to-neuter-or-not-to-neuter dilemma was settled for the time being.

Tuesday morning Mooshie was again missing in action. When the phone rang, I had a pretty good idea who was calling.

"He's here again," Mr. Preston said, bypassing my cheery hello. It was hard to tell if he was pleased or annoyed. "We'd like to introduce Mooshie to Luna this coming weekend if that fits with your schedule. Mrs. Preston is excited about the possibility of having grandkittens. She's making a honeymoon suite for their . . ."

While he searched for a word, I filled in the blank. "Tryst?"

The man cleared his throat. "Ah, yes, that. My wife has furnished the room with pet beds and a cat tree."

"Personally, I think you'd be better off removing the furniture altogether and securing the doors and windows."

The man continued without so much as a chuckle. "If you would have him ready by five on Friday afternoon, I'll pick him up. You'll need at least that much time to prepare him."

"Prepare him? You mean like giving him catnip and telling him about the birds and the bees?"

"I mean that you might want to bulk him up with some good quality red meat. Cats generally don't eat much while they're mating. Petrini's has some nice cuts of prime rib this week."

I thought about the price of prime rib and decided a Burger King quarter-pounder would do just as well.

"Believe me," I said dryly. "If you put on some opera tapes, that will be all the bulking up Mooshie will need."

Elated, I canceled Mooshie's appointment at Snip N' Go.

Friday, at five p.m. sharp, a black Porsche coasted into the driveway and whisked Mooshie away. I lamented that the next time I held him, my sweet little boy would be a full-fledged stud.

*

Late Saturday afternoon I noticed the black Porsche in the Preston parking lot and moseyed over, eager to know if Mooshie had suffered from performance anxiety. The first thing I saw upon entering the parking lot was the dent that extended down the entire left side of the Porsche. The disconcerting notion that Mooshie may have had something to do with the damage stumbled through my mind. I considered turning around and going home, but my curiosity wouldn't let me.

Bob Preston came to the door wearing a neck brace. The sides of his face and his ears were covered with scratches.

"Whoa, what happened to you?"

"Your cat," he winced. "I let him out of the cat carrier before I got out of town thinking that it would make him feel more at ease. He was fine until we got on the freeway. The next thing I know, he's humping the back of my neck. I tried to push him off, but he wouldn't budge. To stabilize himself he sank his claws into my eyebrows which caused me to swerve into the guardrail. I practically went through the windshield."

"Were you singing, or did you have the radio on?"

"You told me he liked opera, so I popped in a CD of famous arias and was singing along, and—"

"And at some point, you hit a B-flat. I should have explained myself. Something about that note affects him— deeply."

"Oh great," Mr. Preston said dryly. "I can't wait to see how my insurance agent works that whimsical morsel of information into the claim."

"How is the honeymoon coming along?" I inquired, hoping to change the subject.

"Resoundingly. Last night the caterwauling was so loud, our neighbors called to complain. We checked on the animals this morning and the place smelled like, well, like a . . ."

"Like a cathouse?" I suggested.

He sighed. "I will say this—if Luna doesn't conceive this time, we're going to have her spayed. We couldn't afford to go through this again."

Regarding me with some intensity, Mr. Preston lowered his voice. "You do know that your cat is a bit mental, right?"

I tried to look as innocent as possible. "Oh? Why do you say that?"

"He jumped onto the breakfast table and started eating the blueberries off my cereal this morning. I went to shoo him off the table but he stared me down and growled while he finished off the berries. It was positively frightening."

I made a mental note to add blueberries to my grocery list then said, "I don't suppose you'd like to hold onto him for another few days to make sure Luna—"

"Not a snowball's chance in hell!" Mr. Preston escorted

me to the door. "Rest assured I'll be bringing him back in one of those steel cages used to transport wild animals."

I was halfway down the walk when I heard the door open behind me.

Mr. Preston stepped outside. "If you want my opinion, I think the breeder sold you an incubus."

I giggled all the way home. The image of my fur-covered incubus humping the back of Bob Preston's neck left me feeling quite fond of my unconventional and horny little demon. I imagined that if my cat were to author an autobiography, he would include a chapter dedicated to his wild weekend with Luna and title it, *Mating Magic with Mooshie: Doin' It Kitty Style!*

The following morning Mooshie was returned to me looking thin and exhausted. For the next two weeks I pampered him with mounds of chicken and tuna and the occasional saucer of English Breakfast tea.

It was at the end of the second week that I caught him staring longingly at my leg again. I let another two weeks pass before stopping by Mr. Preston's office.

He welcomed me inside with a smile.

I skipped the formalities. "Well?"

"Luna will be delivering just before Christmas!" he beamed.

I squealed with joy. I was going to be a grandmother!

Confident that his bloodline would be carried on, I took Mooshie for a ride to the Snip 'N Go—a trip from which he would return permanently altered.

A week later I tested the waters by singing B-flat. From

the absence of dilated pupils and humping, I was sure that Snip 'N Go had done their job well.

Sadly, the fickle finger of fate stepped in to rearrange what seemed like an ideal ending to a happy story. Luna spontaneously aborted in her sixth week of pregnancy and my one shot at grandmotherhood was lost.

At first I was disappointed, but after thinking it through I recognized that it would have been unfair to Mooshie if I'd taken on a second cat. Mooshie was happy being a one-of-a-kind forever cat in a one-cat household.

For as long as he owned me, my cat and I were more than enough for each other.

·6·

ASK NOT FOR WHOM THE BELL TOLLS

"I have studied many philosophers and many cats;
the wisdom of cats is infinitely superior."
— Hippolyte A. Taine (1828 – 1893)

By 1988, things were looking up. My first book, *Intensive Care: The Story of a Nurse,* made it to the *New York Times* bestseller list where it stayed for a couple of months. Even better, I'd signed a contract for a second book, *Mercy.*

During my book tours for *Intensive Care,* it quickly became apparent that I was regarded as a national spokesperson for nurses and healthcare reform. For the majority of my interviews, be it television, radio, or press, the first ninety seconds were devoted to straightforward personal questions—Is that your *real* name? Why did you become a nurse? What led you to write this exposé on what it's like to walk in the shoes of a critical care nurse? The rest of the interview was devoted to fielding questions about the exploitative business of healthcare and how it worked against the nurses' and patients' best interests—all for the sake of profit.

Having served in this capacity for years, I can attest to the fact that being an outspoken whistleblower in the maelstrom of healthcare politics is one of the most fulfilling, frustrating, and frightening things I have ever done.

Thanks to Mooshie, I also had a nice boyfriend who got on well with Simon and didn't mind that I had a writing obsession. The funny thing about our relationship was that Nice Boyfriend and Mooshie had fallen in love before Nice Boyfriend was even aware I existed.

Apparently, my cat was paying attention when I told people that the only way I'd ever meet a potential boyfriend was if he came to the door and knocked, because that is precisely how Mooshie engineered our meeting.

Nice Boyfriend conveniently lived in the fourplex on the opposite side of our parking lot. Mooshie must have observed him coming and going from his downstairs apartment and concluded that the man filled all our requirements: the human male was healthy, he smelled nice, he was without a mate, and he liked cats.

My cat launched into the job of getting the man's attention. According to Nice Boyfriend, "The Mooshmeister" (his name for Mooshie) would creep as close to his apartment door as his leash would allow, then wait for him to emerge from his bachelor cave. To make sure the man noticed him, Mooshie would meow, roll onto his back, and do his Mata Hari wiggle around the blacktop.

Nice Boyfriend, being nice, never failed to pet him and, as might be expected, he soon fell under my cat's spell.

Sensing that the time was right, my cat slipped out of his leash one day and waited on the man's doorstep until he stepped outside. Mooshie then raced for the deadly menace of the busy main thoroughfare. Knowing that Nice Boyfriend would try to rescue him, he allowed himself to be caught and delivered to my front door—and me.

Ours was a love triangle. Mooshie not only commandeered most of Nice Boyfriend's affection, but whenever Nice Boyfriend and I were together, he made sure he was included. At meals, he insisted on being seated at, on, or under the table. If we were sleeping or sitting, he had to be between us.

Though man and beast had a sort of bromance going, Mooshie's true allegiance was with me, his faithful handmaiden. This was evidenced the night Nice Boyfriend and I were sitting close together on the couch. I was busy mending my nursing uniform which had been damaged when an elderly, chemically-altered ER patient ripped off one of the sleeves with his teeth. Nice Boyfriend made a joke about my being ravaged by demented dentures and I laughed so hard, I inadvertently stuck my finger with the needle and squawked.

In a flash Mooshie sprang onto Nice Boyfriend's lap, nipped his hand, then glared at him as if to say, *Make her squawk again, pal, and I'll personally see to it your time here is limited.*

While I was settling into the new relationship, Mooshie

was developing a deep friendship with Jaspurr, his best pal and mentor in all things feline. Life was good for my cat. During the day he had his love fest with Jaspurr, and a few nights a week, Nice Boyfriend's face provided him with a comfy place to sleep. In a state of feline bliss, the tip of Mooshie's pink tongue would poke out of his mouth as the vibrations of Nice Boyfriend's snores lulled him to sleep.

Each morning I'd find Mooshie anxiously waiting by the back door, calling to Jaspurr in a series of chirps and meows. Within minutes Jaspurr would paw or scratch at the door. If the door wasn't opened right away, he'd let loose with one of his gravelly Siamese meows that sounded as if he'd been smoking three packs a day since he was born.

As soon as the door was opened, it was like New Year's Eve in Times Square. Standing on their hind legs, the cat pals would rub noses and fall to the floor, legs entangled. For the next two or three hours, they amused themselves playing hide-and-seek, tag, and ambush, pausing only long enough for water and a snack.

Jaspurr's role as Mooshie's life coach got underway after a friend asked me to take care of her pet rat while she was on her honeymoon. I outright refused, but she was not to be dissuaded. I reminded her that I lived with a cat who was unpredictable when faced with challenges to his natural instincts.

She suggested that having her rat around would be the perfect opportunity to teach my cat self-control.

I persisted, explaining that the very reason I had a cat was to *kill* rats. I warned that bringing her rat to my house would be like putting the hen into the fox den with a sign that read, "Eat me. I'm delicious."

This rationalization did not discourage my friend in the slightest, thus forcing me to divulge the story of why I hated rats with a passion.

When we were kids, my older sister raised hamsters and sold them for a quarter each. I must have a scent that is enticing to rodents, given that as soon as I came within biting range, hoards of the foul-smelling livestock would leave their exercise wheels, bare their hideous front teeth, and bite whichever of my limbs or digits were most accessible. By the time I turned six, I'd probably been relieved of enough blood to transfuse an entire pediatric ward.

I ended my story by telling her that not only would I not trust my cat with her rat, but I wouldn't trust me, either.

My friend rolled her eyes and announced she'd be back with her rat. True to her word, my tenacious friend showed up the next day with the rodent and four boxes of rat accoutrements.

"Garbo loves cats," she assured me. "Don't hesitate to let her interface with Mooshie."

Having seen the way Mooshie tore his fur-covered mice toys to pieces within minutes of receiving them, I was sure any interfacing that might take place would end with a *de-*faced rat.

Several days later, I was in my office when it occurred to me that the rodent's squeaky exercise wheel had been silent for too long. Rushing into the living room, I found

Mooshie and Jaspurr sitting on each side of the rat's cage, the door of which hung open.

Helplessly wriggling under Mooshie's paw, Garbo was issuing squeaks of either terror or laughter—I couldn't tell which.

Jaspurr thumped Mooshie on the head with his paw and my cat let up on the rat. But instead of scurrying back to the safety of her cage, Garbo scampered over, under, and around my cat. Ears twitching, head swiveling, Mooshie followed every move the rodent made with covetous concentration, much like a dog watching the ball before it's thrown. Unable to restrain himself, he caught the rat under his paw, claws unsheathed.

Fast as lightning, Jaspurr cuffed Mooshie's head until he let up on the rat. This scenario was repeated several times before Garbo grew bored and scurried back to her exercise wheel.

Later that evening I let the rodent out of her cage for another interfacing session. Garbo, born without survival instincts, tunneled between Mooshie's front paws. Jaspurr's lesson had taken firm hold in my cat's brain, for after a minute or two of sniffing and fondling, Mooshie allowed her to slither under his belly.

The downside of Jaspurr's rat etiquette tutorial became apparent when real rats of the twelve-inch (not including the tail) Norwegian Viking variety invaded our cottage with the change of season. Besides being huge, these formidable rodents were fearless—and what animal wouldn't be, considering those long incisors that were sharp as razors?

They ate warfarin by the boxful and were all the stronger for it. Electrocution-style traps were a joke. The rats would squeal in orgasmic glee each time one of them stepped on the plate, then leisurely enjoy another tablespoon of peanut butter. Spring-loaded traps were not only sprung but carried away, prize and all.

Mid-afternoon, my concentration and energy waned, necessitating the brewing of a pot of tea. On the way to the kitchen, I passed by my bedroom door and glanced in. Mooshie was sitting in the middle of my four-poster canopy bed, looking up.

After years of observing my fellow humans, one of the many things I found puzzling was that without a specific intention such as looking at the stars or checking the sky for rain, humans rarely look up. Following human nature, I didn't look up either. Instead, I focused on my cat and stroked his head. Rather than climbing onto my shoulder or curling up in my lap, he dodged my hand and pushed it away with his paw. Then he went back to looking up.

So, I looked up.

The scream that followed was so loud, I was sure I'd damaged my vocal cords. Directly above us, balancing on the canopy slats, was the largest rodent I'd ever seen.

Grabbing Mooshie I made for the door, but before I could get into the hallway, my cat wiggled out of my arms, jumped back onto the bed, and recommenced looking up. I scooped him off the bed and again, he jumped out of my arms and ducked under the bed.

It occurred to me then that Mooshie equated Ratzilla

with Garbo the pet rat, and thought he could have some gentle "interfacing time" with a rodent that could cause my cat serious harm. I took another look at the wharf rat and ran for the phone.

I called Lindo and insisted he evict Ratzilla asap.

Lindo laughed and was chiding me for making such a fuss over a "little mouse," when from the bedroom there came a loud crash followed by a thud.

I cracked open my bedroom door and peered inside. Mooshie was balancing on one of the narrow canopy slats while directly below, Ratzilla sat on the bed, waiting for my cat to fall.

Lindo arrived five minutes later, still laughing.

He peeked over my shoulder, made the sign of the cross and whispered, "Holy Mother of God!" Without another word, he went to his truck and returned attired in canvas overalls, heavy work gloves, safety goggles, and a hardhat. He carried a formidable sledgehammer in one hand and a duffle bag in the other. He took a deep breath, entered the room, and closed the door behind him.

There was banging, grunts, and a string of curses that even *I* hadn't heard before. Thirty minutes later, Lindo exited the bedroom pale and perspiring. His shirt was torn and there were blood spatters on the legs of his overalls. In solemn triumph, he nodded toward the duffle bag which appeared to have been packed with a couple of bowling balls.

I sent Lindo off with a pan of homemade zucchini bread and steeled myself for the worst before I entered the bedroom. My shoes were flung haphazardly all about the room, and there was a hole the size of a sledgehammer head in the closet floor.

Unperturbed, Mooshie sat on my pillow, cleaning his claws. I examined every inch and claw and found him unscathed. Thankful that both my cat and my house survived with only minimal damage and mess, I breathed a sigh of relief.

My sense of relief was short-lived. Not long after the Ratzilla incident, I arrived home from work one night and the first thing I noticed as I drove into the parking lot was a weird flickering light coming from my living room windows. As I got closer, I saw that it wasn't so much a flickering as it was a swinging rhythm: bright light, shadow, bright light, shadow, and so on.

I parked and rested my forehead on the steering wheel, reciting Dorothy Parker's famous line: "What fresh hell is this?"

My evening shift in the ER had been downright atrocious. Dealing with the aftermath of people's frailties, inhumanity, and ignorance had drained me of my tolerance for any sort of chicanery. All night I'd been counting on coming home to a quiet house, a hot shower, and snuggling up with my cat.

That tranquil vision dissolved upon my discovery of Nice Boyfriend and Joni sitting in the porch rocking chairs like it was a lovely summer's afternoon at the nursing home, rather than a damp and frigid November midnight.

I pointed to my front door. "Should I even bother to ask what's going on in there?"

"That's what we'd like to know," Nice Boyfriend replied. "We couldn't find your house key where you usually hide it—you know, the secret hiding place that everyone in Marin County knows about?"

"Sorry. I moved it and then forgot where I hid it."

"Jaspurr didn't come home tonight," Joni said. "I'm pretty sure he's in there with Mooshie. We pressed our ears against the bay windows and heard strange sounds."

"Yeah," murmured Nice Boyfriend under his breath. "Like heavy falling objects."

With Joni and Nice Boyfriend behind me, I unlocked the door. The moment it swung open, Jaspurr shot out between our feet. From the way his ears lay back and the speed at which he fled, it appeared to be a run-for-your-life escape.

Joni backed off the porch. "That's enough for me. I'm going home to check my cat for head injuries."

"Oh come on," I pleaded. "Aren't you dying to know what's going on in there?"

"Nope. From the way my cat came out of there, I can only imagine what you'll discover this time, and I don't want to see it up close."

Nice Boyfriend and I waited in the hallway, listening to the barely audible creaking sound that matched the rhythm of the light and shadow show. Unable to hold off any longer, I braced myself and stepped into the living room.

We stood wide-eyed, taking it all in. Before us lay devastation that rivaled the aftermath of a Canadian hockey game brawl—minus the blood. The couch cover was wadded into a ball in the corner, and the braided rug was shoved partway into the kitchen. My antique brass floor lamp lay at an odd angle against the window seat. The bare bulb, caught in the lace curtains, had scorched a hole through both panels. The lampshade had come to rest atop the piano, and the pile of sheet music that I kept there was scattered from one end of the living room to the other. Both ceramic flower vases, last seen on the mantle, lay in pieces on the floor. The water from said vases had mixed with the fireplace ashes to form a black slurry. Black pawprints covered every surface, including the couch and the window seat cushions.

I reluctantly turned my eyes to the ceiling.

There, resembling a demented howler monkey, Mooshie hung by his claws from one side of Perch And Twirl's cage. Each of his attempts to gain purchase made the cage swing in a wide arc, rhythmically blocking and unblocking the light from the bare bulb. The scene that came to mind was from the 1933 *King Kong* movie where Kong hangs by one hand from the peak of the Empire State Building, batting at the planes.

It didn't seem to make a bit of difference to Mooshie that he'd been caught in the act of trying to kill the canary, considering that he continued eyeing the bird while making his chattery pre-kill sounds.

We were never able to figure out how he managed to reach a cage that hung from the center of the high ceiling, but now that my cat had acquired a taste for the hunt, I reckoned Perch And Twirl would not survive the trauma of repeated assassination attempts.

Joni, I decided, was going to love her new canary.

*

The Perch And Twirl debacle provided Nice Boyfriend with the incentive he needed to begin the Free Mooshie campaign. According to him, the Mooshmeister was desperate to roam the world without any interference from me or his leash.

In retrospect, I'm pretty sure this was a case of Nice Boyfriend projecting his own desire for freedom onto Mooshie. I compromised by extending Mooshie's leash another twenty-five feet. This would take him to within twenty feet of the main street in one direction and to the middle of the creek in the other.

On our first warm spring day, I put Mooshie on his extended leash and settled in one of the porch chairs with a pen and writing pad. I'd written one paragraph when my cat jumped onto the trunk of the 1961 Mercury Comet convertible parked next to our Chevy.

Virginia, the Mercury's elderly owner, lived in Right Bank Cottage #4. A celebrity in her own right, she, along with Aldous Huxley, had been among the first to test Dr. Albert Hofmann's Special Cure-All, better known as Lysergic Acid Diethylamide—LSD for short.

The tough old bird's exact age was a frequent topic of discussion among the cottagers, as we were pretty sure she'd been alive and kicking during the First World War.

Metaphorically speaking, the Mercury had about the same mileage on it as its owner, but it looked a whole lot better: the chrome gleamed, the paint was pristine, and the black ragtop had never once been down.

Being the heat-seeking creature he was, once Mooshie discovered that the black ragtop could absorb enough heat to fry eggs, he considered it his private slice of heaven—or hell, depending on how one looked at it.

I watched my cat make his way to the ragtop and roll around in heat-mongering ecstasy. He then stretched out and without any further preparation, fell asleep in the center of the roof. No more than thirty minutes later, Virginia, a cigarette dangling from her lips, hobbled by to take her classic roadster down to Jolly King Liquors to purchase her weekly carton of unfiltered Pall Malls.

One eye squinted against the cigarette smoke, the old lady leaned on her cane and regarded the feline sleeping beauty. Without ceremony, she scooped him up with one bony hand and lowered him to the ground.

Mooshie eyed her feet. Chances are she'd had prior dealings with his teeth on account of how fast the old woman scrambled to get into the car before he could attack. Slowed by age, arthritis, and a bum hip, she didn't make it. Mooshie threw himself onto her Oxfords and nipped at the elastic stockings that held her varicose veins in place. She shook him off, but by the time she got inside the vehicle, Mooshie was back on the ragtop.

The old lady shouted at him through the window and started the motor.

Nice bluff, I thought. Mooshie must have been thinking the same thing because he settled in, his tail switching in a lazy, devil-may-care sort of way.

The backup lights flickered to life and the car slowly reversed. I held my breath, debating whether or not to intervene in this test of wills between an old lady and a stubborn cat.

Never believing for an instant that Virginia would endanger my cat's life, I checked my impulse to run over and remove Mooshie from her roof. I was sure that once he understood Virginia was calling his bluff, he would concede defeat and jump off.

Not a chance.

Virginia's arm snaked out the window to take a few blind swings at her new roof ornament. In turn, Mooshie yawned and raised himself enough to take a few swipes at her hand—to let her know he was calling her bluff.

The old lady braked, put the Mercury in drive, and . . . drove away.

I sprinted to the car, reaching the back bumper with only two feet of slack left on the leash. Just before the car moved out from under him, I nabbed the leash and pulled my cat off the ragtop and into my arms. His expression was one of sheer incredulity as he gaped at Virginia's disappearing tailpipe.

Jaspurr, having witnessed the whole thing from a safe distance, sauntered up to Mooshie and, after sniffing him all over, licked the top of his head as if to say, *Don't mess with the old ladies—they're tough.*

I found Joni working in her garden and had just finished relating the crazy driveway scene when our cats sauntered into the yard. Spying some terrible threat, Mooshie froze then crouched behind a single blade of grass, readying himself for the lunge. His intended victim—a dead maple leaf—fluttered in the breeze, taunting him.

The intensity of his focus clearly broadcast what was going on in his mind: *I'm totally invisible behind this blade of grass and I've got the target in sight. I'm tensing, I'm wiggling, I'm wiggling, I'm . . . duh, wait—what comes next?*

Joni squinted. "What is he doing?"

"He's trying to remember how to attack that ferocious dead leaf."

Joni snapped her fingers at Jaspurr. "Sic him!"

Jaspurr leaped, wrapping one foreleg around Mooshie's neck in the feline version of a half nelson. Mooshie nipped at the Siamese's ears until the usual game of tag was in full swing.

"I'm pretty sure my cat thinks of your cat as a younger, developmentally delayed brother," Joni speculated. "Mooshie's lack of the basics is Jaspurr's call to duty."

I nodded, recalling the Siamese's tutoring efforts on proper feline outdoor toilet technique. Joni and I were familiar with Mooshie's strange though diligent process of preparing the receiving hole: digging, sniffing, then rejecting hole after hole. It took a few months of coaching, but Jaspurr finally trained him to dig careless holes (two scoops at most), squat, produce some used cat food, then in the slapdash manner of an afterthought kick a thin spray of dirt over the mound and walk away.

The problem was that as soon as Mooshie grasped the idea that he didn't need to be so tidy in his toileting, his pendulum swung with fiendish intent to the far side of sloppy. Demonstrating (emphasis on the first five letters of that word) his ability to understand humans, Mooshie came up with a new trick. Every time—not some of the time—but *every* time company came to the door, whether it was a planned or a spontaneous visit, he would greet the humans at the door with enthusiastic chirps of welcome and endearing shows of affection.

Winding his tail around their legs and ankles, he would conduct them into the house, chirping and purring while basking in the usual accolades of, "Oh what a sweet little kitty!"

As soon as they were comfortably seated, Mooshie would run to his litterbox with an urgency that implied, *Thank God you came when you did!* and then deposit the foulest-smelling intestinal creation ever produced in feline history. As if that wasn't bad enough, my cat added auditory insult to olfactory injury by expressing himself (so to speak) with resonant, human-like grunts and squeals while thus engaged.

I do not exaggerate when I say the odor sent my guests scurrying outside, gagging. He never once attempted to cover the offending bundles. He gave new meaning to the witch's line in Macbeth that "something wicked this way comes."

Anyone who dared brave a second visit to our cottage usually brought gifts of scented candles or incense. The less subtle among them either doused themselves in perfume or coated the insides of their nostrils with Vicks VapoRub.

*

The debate among animal behaviorists as to whether animals experience emotions is, in my humble opinion, a no-brainer. Cats are sensitives. They intuit things that are out of reach for most of us imperceptive humans. Cats sense subtle changes in all manner of things, from the moods of humans to a disaster that is taking place many miles away. At first sniff, cats know the true nuts and bolts of a being's spirit and, if it is broken or injured, most cats will attempt to comfort.

The Monday before Thanksgiving, Jaspurr arrived on time for his standing playdate with Mooshie. I noticed that after their initial greeting of nose kisses, Mooshie was uncharacteristically subdued. Their normally energetic rough-and-tumble play was abandoned in favor of Mooshie giving Jaspurr's face and ears a lick-bath.

I checked on them thirty minutes later and found Mooshie standing over his friend in a protective stance, watching him sleep. I thought it strange, but reasoned that cats are mercurial creatures; like humans, they have their good and bad days.

I'd been writing for about an hour when Mooshie came in and jumped into my lap. This was odd given that whenever Jaspurr was in the house Mooshie only had eyes for him. If I showed affection to the Siamese, Mooshie would get between us and shove my hand away—Jaspurr was his and no one else could horn in on their time together.

"What is it, Buddha Man? Where's your pal?"

In answer, Mooshie voiced his concern in staccato chirps and meows, desperate to communicate whatever was bothering him. He went into the hall and turned back to look at me. In expression and attitude, my cat did a perfect imitation of Lassie anxiously barking the message that Timmy had fallen down the well once again and needed saving.

Mooshie led me to the forced-air wall heater where Jaspurr lay on his side taking the heat full blast. That alone was noteworthy since Jaspurr was not a heat-seeking type of cat. Moving him away from the heater, I was shocked at how weak he was.

I did a quick assessment, recalling the day when the ailing Siamese strayed into Joni's life. The vet who treated him told her that Jaspurr had a rare blood disorder that would most certainly shorten his lifespan.

With Mooshie on my heels, I carried Jaspurr to Joni's cottage.

She met me at the door. "I was afraid of this," she said, her voice filled with despair. "I knew something was wrong when he didn't eat this morning, but I was hoping his visit with Mooshie would give him an appetite. I'll take him to the vet, but I don't think they can do much more for him."

For the next two days my cat sat by the back door waiting for his best friend to arrive. Every so often he would sniff at the crack under the door then intone the three-note come-play-with-me call he'd learned from Jaspurr.

Thanksgiving morning I awoke to find Mooshie sitting

on the window seat, staring out at Joni and Jaspurr's cottage. I stroked his head and repeated the word tuna a few times, but he was so far into his misery it was like I wasn't even there. For the rest of the morning, and until I left for work, he did not budge from the window.

Thanksgiving is one of the busiest nights in an emergency department, so I didn't get home until after two a.m. Instead of greeting me at the door, Mooshie was still on the window seat keeping vigil for Jaspurr.

I gathered up my cat and brought him into bed with me. "What's going on, Moosh? Are you worried about Jaspurr? Do you want to visit him tomorrow? How about if I call Joni in the morning and see if you can visit?"

Dog-like, Mooshie put his head on my chest.

At 4:14 a.m. I awoke to the sound of Mooshie's cries. I found him anxiously pacing in front of the bay windows. Petting, tuna, and even a handful of potato chips held no attraction for him. Not knowing what else to do, I spoke to him in soothing undertones, promising that everything was going to be okay.

But of course, it wasn't okay. When the phone rang at seven a.m., I knew the news was not going to be good.

"He's gone," Joni whispered.

I glanced over at Mooshie who was still staring desolately out the window. No longer standing at attention, he was lying down, his head resting on his foreleg.

I threw on my slippers and hurried down to the cottage of mourning, where I made hot tea and toast for my other heartbroken friend.

"He couldn't get warm," Joni began. "I curled up with him in front of the heater, and then he . . . he stopped breathing."

"Was that around quarter after four this morning?"

Joni nodded. "How—?"

"Mooshie woke me up with his distress calls. He wouldn't leave the window facing your cottage."

Speaking softly, Joni looked down at her hands. "You know, when Jaspurr strayed into my yard three years ago all beaten up and thin as a cracker, he knew he'd found his true home. He was so *grateful* for everything—every meal, every treat, every hug and—" She covered her face and cried.

"Could you come back in an hour or so?" she said, not taking her hands from her face. "I need more time."

Mooshie was still on the windowsill watching me like a hawk as I walked back to our cottage. I held him close while he sniffed my robe and face, looking for confirmation of what he instinctively knew.

While I dressed, Mooshie sat on the bed waiting to be cuddled. I picked him up and kissed his head, murmuring how much I loved him. Though he was just out of his teens in cat years, the thought that this precious feline soul would also die someday presented itself as an unwanted guest. Unbidden, the first line of Yehuda Halevi's poem went through my head over and over like an LED banner: *'Tis a fearful thing to love what death can touch.*

I banished the thought, unwilling to entertain even the possibility of Mooshie ever dying. Besides, that was a long way off in the future.

Before I left the house I put Mooshie in the bathroom,

making sure the window was securely shut. I didn't want him to witness the burial of his friend.

Joni and I buried Jaspurr along with his squeaky toys and a favorite tinfoil ball, under an arbor of roses.

For the two days Mooshie was kept inside, he sat on the window seat staring at Jaspurr's cottage. On the third day, I let him out on his leash. He sat in the middle of the path for a while then walked to the spot where we'd buried Jaspurr. He sniffed the ground before coming to a standstill directly over his friend's resting place.

I stroked his head until he moved away, letting me know he wanted to be left alone. I sat with Joni on her porch watching the clouds until she broke the silence.

"It's amazing, isn't it?" she said. "Mooshie *knew* right where his best buddy was. He knew—" Her voice broke.

On cue, Mooshie entered the yard and jumped into Joni's lap unbidden—a thing he'd never done before. Clutching him to her, she wept in the way of those who have been left behind by a loved pet.

In his infinite wisdom, Mooshie allowed her to grieve for as long as she needed.

*

Three things happened simultaneously after Jaspurr's death that again led me out into the world. First, I received a warning from the nursing office that either I use my stockpile of paid vacation time or lose it altogether. Then, a friend living on St. John invited me and a companion to come for a visit and stay in his guest house. The day after I received this invite, Joni, still deep in her grief, told me she wanted to get away and asked if I would be up for taking a trip somewhere.

If I wanted more convincing to take a vacation, all I had to do was consider that I desperately needed a break from my work at the hospital, Nice Boyfriend and I needed a break from each other, and Mooshie and Nice Boyfriend both hoped I'd go away so they could hang out and snore to their hearts' content.

Not wanting to look a whole herd of gift horses in the mouth, I was determined to go to St. John and relax. A few weeks later, armed with sunscreen, bathing suits, and plenty of reading material, Joni and I headed to the U.S. Virgin Islands.

Within a few days of arriving on St. John, my friend arranged for Joni and me to fly with a friend of his to Montserrat, the Emerald Isle of the Caribbean. Upon landing, I opened the aircraft's door and stepped out onto the wing. Without forethought or expectation, I was inexplicably filled with a sense that I was finally home.

We ended up staying for two weeks in a lovely house that the pilot was temporarily caretaking. Tucked away in the tropical forest, I fell under the island's magical spell. The evening before I returned to St. John, I was walking along the waterfront asking for a sign that I would someday return to the island. At the very instant the sun slipped below the horizon, a blaze of neon green light lit up the sky.

On our return trip, a fellow passenger told me this rare occurrence was the legendary green flash, once known as the Emerald Drop. According to the local folklore, the person who was fortunate enough to witness it was bound to revisit the island.

The very thought that I might return to Montserrat someday gave me a sense of hope and joy. It triggered a memory of my sixth Christmas when I received a paint-by-number set. The two canvases were of a palm-lined beach and a tropical rainforest. When the paintings were finished, I hung them on my bedroom wall. Every morning I would wake to those scenes and pray that someday I would live in just such a place.

I had no idea how, when, or even if I could ever make that happen, but now that I'd found the island, it was something I could dream about.

PART TWO

LIFE IN THE TIME OF ABSCESSES

·7·
RELEASE THE KRAKEN!

"Of all God's creatures, there is only one that cannot be made a slave of the leash. That one is the cat."

— Mark Twain (1835 – 1910)

Every October I would trek over the Golden Gate bridge to attend the annual San Francisco Cat Exhibition. This exhibition is to me what a Green Bay Packers Super Bowl game is to a Cheesehead.

Besides the cats, the main draws of a cat show are the new lines of cat toys and gimmicks. Take, for instance, videos for cats. At the time these VHS tapes first came out, I scoffed at the idea that any self-respecting cat would think the birds and fish on the screen were real. The more I thought about it, the more I wondered how Mooshie might react. The price was a bit steep, but I purchased one anyway and brought it home.

I rented a VCR player, hooked it up to a borrowed

television, and waited until Mooshie settled on the window seat for a nap. I then called in Nice Boyfriend and Joni to witness my cat's reactions.

Mooshie's wheezy snores were my cue to start the tape and turn up the volume. The video opened on an outdoor aviary filled with ten or so finches chirping, flying, eating, and generally having as nice a time as birds can have inside an aviary.

Within seconds, Mooshie's ears went twitchy. He jumped down from the window seat and sat in front of the treadle sewing machine cabinet upon which the TV rested. At the next burst of bird chatter, his pupils dilated and his head jerked rapidly side to side as he tracked the movements of the frolicking birds. His chin began to quiver and his urgent *keh! keh! keh!* cries sounded like the feline version of *Oh my God, look at them all!*

He crept closer to the sewing machine, accidentally stepped on the treadle pedal, and launched himself backward. Recovering with no sign of embarrassment, he jumped onto the cabinet and sniffed the sides of the TV, then edged around to the back to peer inside the air slots.

He then climbed on top of the set searching the ceiling for any birds that might have escaped. Finding none, Mooshie returned to the floor and resumed scrutinizing the onscreen birds until his eyes glazed over—as if he were in a post-orgasmic reverie.

I was about to turn off the video when Mooshie suddenly sprang into the air and hit the television screen, teeth first. He jumped again, this time clapping his paws together against the screen as if to clasp one of the birds and bring it down with him. Landing, he studied his empty front paws and then the ceiling, incredulous that there was no bird.

In a decent imitation of a Hare Krishna devotee, the jumping went on with few variations in style until he was jumping apparently just for the love of jumping—sometimes facing the TV, sometimes facing the opposite wall.

Certain that my cat's jumping jamboree was the best in comedy, I invited a few Left and Right Bank neighbors over for the live entertainment. Instead of finding Mooshie uproariously funny, my bemused neighbors left the cottage one by one shaking their heads, no doubt trying to decide whom they should call first—the SPCA or mental health services.

Joni and Nice Boyfriend stayed behind for the sole purpose of implementing an intervention on Mooshie's behalf. Sitting on either side of me, the two employed a tag-team approach.

Joni went first: "Have you ever thought about letting Mooshie off his leash?"

"Yeah," Nice Boyfriend chimed in, "The Mooshmeister should have the freedom to check out other neighborhoods, make new friends, catch a few bir—"

". . . big rats." Joni cut in, quick to banish any thought that my feline Mahatma Gandhi might kill a bird. "He misses Jaspurr. He's lonely. If he could run free and explore the neighborhood, he might find a new friend."

"Oh sure," I muttered. "Like a rabid raccoon or a pissed off rattlesnake?"

Joni pondered this for a moment then said, "The added benefit of letting him loose is that he'll bulk up and learn self-defense. He's so small and—"

"Wimpish," Nice Boyfriend finished for her.

"Burmese are a naturally compact breed," I protested. "Plus, the main street is at the end of our driveway. He'll make a beeline for it as soon as he realizes he's free."

Joni rolled her eyes. "He's not *that* stupid."

I raised an eyebrow and glanced over at Mooshie still jumping at the television screen.

Nice Boyfriend, who was only too aware of Mooshie's death-defying history with street traffic, nodded. "We'll take turns training him to avoid the street, I promise."

"Right," Joni agreed. "And he'll come home when he's called."

I regarded them warily, skeptical of their arguments. But then I caught sight of my cat jumping at the screen with mindless joy and the first twinge of guilt made me hesitate.

"I don't know. The poor little guy already works so hard to, um . . ." I faltered. "Adjust?"

Nice Boyfriend laughed. "The hardest work the Mooshmeister has ever done is to empty his bladder, move his bowels, and find ways to boost his nutritional intake. And the only thing he ever had to adjust to was the time his food bowl was mistakenly placed on the left side of his water bowl instead of the right."

I felt terrible. Maybe it *was* cruel to keep an animal indoors or on a leash for his whole life. I thought of zoos and my lifelong dislike of them. I envisioned despondent animals pacing back and forth in their cages, peering out from behind bars, never to roam free. Would letting Mooshie have his freedom for a few hours a day really be so bad?

Then I remembered Dr. Petrie's lectures on indoor vs. outdoor cats. I intoned the vet's favorite mantra: "Indoor cats live longer and are happier, healthier animals."

"Do you honestly believe the Mooshmeister is happier locked up inside all the time like a *prisoner*?" Nice Boyfriend glared at me like I was a Nazi war criminal. "Even when the Mooshmeister is outside he's tied up with all these ropes and harnesses like some kind of *animal*!"

"He *is* an animal," I pointed out.

"I feel bad for him," Joni added. "He's always in the window gazing out, longing to run free in the fresh air and sunshine."

The theme song from *Born Free* played in the background of my mind.

"Jeez, I don't know. Maybe—"

"I'll look out for him," Joni promised, driving wedges of false security into my cracking resolve. "We'll all watch over him. He'll be our communal kitty."

"But there are some things about being on the leash that Mooshie likes," I insisted.

"Name one," they chorused.

"Well, how about the fact that he really likes being taken out for a drag?"

Nice Boyfriend frowned. "What does that mean . . . 'a drag'?"

"Have you seen that old lady who walks down Miller Avenue every day with her cat on a leash?"

Joni and Nice Boyfriend wore identical blank expressions.

"I stopped her one day to ask about her cat and she told me that he genuinely enjoys walking on the leash. So, I thought I'd give it a try with Mooshie. I waited for a nice day, clipped his short leash onto his harness, and headed for the street. The second Mooshie felt the pull on his harness, he fell over onto his side and let me drag him. I'd put him back on his feet, but he kept flopping onto his side.

"I dragged him for about ten feet thinking he'd get up, but instead, he started purring and got that glassy-eyed look he gets when you rub under his chin.

"Every thirty feet or so, he'd get to his feet, shake himself off, flop down on his other side, and wait for me to drag him again. Ever since then, whenever he sees me approach with the short leash he automatically flops onto his side and starts purring. We've been around the block a half dozen times that way.

"Sure, people look at us oddly, but as long as Mooshie is happy, I don't care."

"They probably think you're some psycho who's dragging a trussed-up dead cat around town. You need to give the Mooshmeister a chance at being a *normal* cat. He needs to build up some street cred—let the poor bastard have some dignity. At the very least, the neighbors will have to stop calling him The Cat on a Rope."

Mooshie chose that moment to jump into my lap and meow in his most forlorn voice. My shoulders slumped in defeat. I tried to smile, but in my head all I could hear was Zeus's command in *Clash of the Titans*: "Release the Kraken!"

*

A few days later I carried my cat, sans harness and ropes, outside and sat him down under the plum tree. I got on my hands and knees and looked him squarely in the eye.

"Listen up, Moosh. I'm going to let you explore on your own, but you must promise that the minute you hear me calling for you, you'll come right away and not make me worry. Most important, you cannot go near the street." I pointed to the busy street.

Mooshie looked in the direction in which my finger pointed then back at me. He blinked as if to say, *Duh. You must think I'm an imbecile.*

"I trust you to be the cat I've raised you to be, which is to say, totally dependent on me."

Realizing that something momentous was about to take place, my cat chirped impatiently. I steeled myself and walked away without a backward glance—until I got to the porch, where I spun around and watched his every move.

Mooshie had already found a patch of dirt and was flopping around like a breakdancer out of his mind on amphetamines. After finishing his dirt bath, he sauntered in the direction of the creek, stopping at Jaspurr's grave for a moment of kitty homage. Then, as if possessed, he zoomed up the fig tree, jumped down, ran around in circles, and disappeared, ears flattened to his head.

I sighed. The Kraken had been released upon the unsuspecting world.

*

When I am in the process of writing, I dissociate and ignore all reality that might be going on around me. It's like I'm in an empty soundproof theater, completely involved in whatever scene is taking place on the stage inside my mind. I consider it a mixed blessing that this ability to block out the rest of the world did not apply when it came to Mooshie.

On the fourth day of the Outdoor Cat Freedom Ride, things went a little wonky when Mooshie didn't return home within five minutes of being called in for dinner. I went back to my writing thinking that if he wasn't home within the hour, I'd call Joni to help me search the neighborhood.

Forty-five minutes later I was assaulted by a stench so disgusting I held my breath for fear of breathing in some alien spore deadly enough to kill me on the spot. The screen door creaked and the putrid odor grew stronger. I held a sweatshirt over my nose and mouth and stepped into the hall.

Proud as a peacock, Mooshie sat by the front door slicked down with slimy muck. He voiced a string of cheery chirps and meows and tried to jump into my arms.

I backed into the bathroom, plugged the sink, turned on the taps, and waited for curiosity to pull my cat in. The moment he stepped into the bathroom, I closed the door behind him. He took one look at the cat shampoo bottle and flew under the clawfoot tub. I lunged for his hind legs and pulled him out, his front claws scraping the linoleum.

As I lowered him closer to the water, all four legs shot out and hooked onto the edges of the sink—exactly like in the cartoons. At the last second before his body made contact with the water, he slipped out of my hands and again disappeared under the tub.

Twenty minutes later he was wheezing and I was bleeding from multiple scratches. In the name of self-preservation, I resorted to sponging the gore and muck from my cat's fur. So much for my conviction that cats were the tidiest animals on earth.

We repeated this gymnastic exercise several times until I was sure one of us was going to have a heart attack. The next time he came home stinking to high heaven, I figured that since Mooshie was a heat monger, instead of the recommended tepid water, I'd fill the sink with hot water, dialed down a notch or two.

Sniffing the steam rising from the sink, he dipped in one paw, and then the other. For incentive, I threw in a ping-pong ball. A few minutes later he was submerged up to his neck, one elbow resting on the sink rim. With his free paw he played at trying to drown the ping-pong ball by pushing it under the water, then releasing it so it would spring back up for recapture. I could almost hear him thinking, *Ah, this is the life—after a hard night of rolling around in dead animal guts I come home to a hot bath, a game of ping pong, and a servant who rubs me down and gives me fresh tuna!*

In hindsight, the arduous bath routine was child's play compared with the Kraken's unfortunate next phase, which we dubbed: Life in the Time of Abscesses.

In a unique twist on the practice of gunmen carving notches in their gun belts for every outlaw they shot, Mooshie started collecting ear notches for every fight he lost. Not content to settle for an ear notch or two, my cat moved on to adventures in dental destruction. During this phase, he lost a premolar and one incisor, broke a lower canine in half, and chipped his snaggletooth. Instead of the "bulking up" he was supposed to be doing, my cat was paring down body part by body part.

Mooshie must have had an itch to revisit his suicide fantasies because he upped his game. At least once every six weeks Mooshie the feline pincushion would show up sporting a new puncture wound, in which an abscess would eventually fester. By the third abscess, I suggested to Dr. Petrie that he should just give me his mortgage information and tell me where to send the monthly payments.

Mooshie's experiments with anatomical rearrangement came to a head the night he limped into the house with a flap of skin hanging from his hind leg. That wound and the subsequent hospitalizations and surgeries needed to repair it put a major damper on his bravado. Adding insult to injury, Dr. Petrie requested permission to use photographs of Mooshie's injuries for an anti-outdoor-cat poster he was creating for his waiting room.

For Mooshie, a.k.a The Kraken, his convalescence gave him plenty of time to reflect on his failed efforts to build up "street cred" with the neighborhood wildlife. In his autobiography, I'm sure he would have added this phase of his life in a chapter titled, *Letters from Cage 12: An Insider's View of Pet Hospitals.*

He must have concluded that it would be best for all involved if he threw in the towel and retired the Kraken alter ego. He didn't roam too far after that, preferring instead to stay close to the cottage where he felt safe.

Excuse me while I reflect on the irony of that last sentence.

*

A few minutes before 5:04 p.m. on October 17, 1989, I was cooking spaghetti sauce, thinking about what a beautiful day it was.

Mooshie crouched at my feet, wiggled his hindquarters, and flew into my arms. He placed both forelegs around my neck and touched his muzzle to my lips before draping himself over my shoulder.

He'd been particularly clingy all day; following on my heels every time I moved and voicing an endless stream of chirpy jabberwocky, as if he'd experienced a traumatic psychological setback and needed to work it through.

In response to his meows and chirps, I imitated my therapist, murmuring standard shrink phrases: "Hmmm, it sounds like your inner critic is sabotaging you again," or, "Let's get in touch with your inner kitten, shall we?"

The front screen door squeaked open. Mooshie launched himself off my shoulder and skidded into the entrance hall. A few seconds later Nice Boyfriend appeared with Mooshie slung casually over his shoulder. He kissed me hello and started explaining that he was home early so that he could catch game three of the World Series between the Oakland Athletics and the San Francisco Giants.

All at once everything came into sharp focus—the perfect weather, my wonderful unconventional cat, my nice boyfriend, my good life. The simple pleasures of life overwhelmed me and I burst into tears.

Mooshie and Nice Boyfriend gaped at me as if I'd sprouted a set of antlers. I rarely cry, so I was as shocked as they were by the sudden flood of tears. Nice Boyfriend, thinking that I was either having a heart attack or a mental breakdown, carried me to my bed. Mooshie jumped onto my chest, anxiously sniffing my face and hands, trying to determine what was wrong with his main serving wench.

In the same instant I reached for my cat to reassure him that I'd not gone mental, Mooshie's eyes dilated and his fur stood up on end along his spine to the tip of his tail in a kind of kitty Mohawk. Ears laid back, he flew off the bed and into the hall. The screen door banged open and my cat exited the cottage stage right.

Nice Boyfriend laughed. "What the hell was *that* all ab—"

The low rumble seemed to come from the middle of the earth. I'd heard the sound enough times in my twenty-two years in California to recognize it at once as the heralding drumroll of an earthquake—except this rumble was louder and more pronounced than anything I'd previously encountered.

Out in the hallway, our twenty-pound mirror swung on its hooks.

"Run to the middle of the parking lot," I yelled, pushing Nice Boyfriend to the bedroom door.

"Oh come on, Ec. This is nothing. It's only a minor qua—"

My office desk slid into the hallway.

Arguing with Nice Boyfriend from Connecticut over how little he knew about earthquakes was trumped by my excitement that the "Big One" I'd been waiting twenty-two years for had finally arrived.

The cottage rocked side to side on its foundation. When my office bookcases toppled over with a resounding crash, I pulled Nice Boyfriend outside onto the undulating blacktop of the parking lot. My gaze bounced continuously from the overhead power lines to the fissures that were appearing under our feet. I saw nothing of Mooshie but felt confident that being a cat, he'd seek safety down by the creek, away from the buildings and overhead lines.

I turned to tell Nice Boyfriend to watch for falling power lines, only to discover he was no longer behind me. What I did see was our cottage shaking and swaying like a giant pink elephant struggling to get free of its foundation. The screen door swung open and closed with each roll of the earth.

I rushed into the rocking cottage fully expecting to find Nice Boyfriend crushed under the hallway mirror. Instead, I found him in the bedroom doorway crouched protectively around Mooshie.

I took hold of both man and beast and retreated to the parking lot. Sandwiched between his two most ardent devotees, Mooshie's heart was beating hard and fast. While the earth pitched under us, we petted him, murmuring in low voices not to be afraid.

Mooshie did not leave my shoulder until I fell into bed that night. There he lay on my chest and fixed his gaze on mine. I interpreted his expression as, *I'm glad I saved the lives of my trusty handmaiden and my personal valet today, but if it happens again, you're on your own.*

When I look back on the Loma Prieta earthquake, I like to think that Mooshie, acting out of love for his support staff, had returned to the cottage to find us so we could face the disaster together.

·8·

THE CAT WHO WOULD BE KING

"I have lived with several Zen masters—
all of them cats."

— Eckhart Tolle, *The Power of Now*

Mooshie was still off leash, but he'd moved on from anatomical mutilation and into what we referred to as his "Houdini in the Used Car Lot" phase of life.

In Mooshie's case the old idiom-proverb, "curiosity killed the cat" was particularly befitting. Nothing escaped his investigation. While his extreme need-to-know mindset often led to entertaining results, there were times when his investigational skills led him into trouble. Take, for instance, his complex relationship with motor vehicles.

From the time he was a kitten, he'd been on overly-friendly terms with vehicles. Despite being rudely jerked from the rag roof of Virginia's Mercury, his fascination with, and his cavalier attitude toward cars and trucks, was not in any way diminished.

Enter Pablo, the Left and Right Banks' odd-jobber guy. Pablo performed all the dangerous and dirty jobs that Lindo didn't care to deal with, like roof repair, reaming out the sewer pipes, and anything having to do with electricity.

One afternoon as Pablo was getting into his truck, I noticed Mooshie sitting directly in the middle of the parking lot, grooming himself. I stepped forward to move my cat out of the path of Pablo's vehicle when the man waved me away. "*Por favor Señora*—let *El Gato* stay as he is."

"But there's no room for your truck to get around him, Pablo."

"*Sí,* this is true, but *El Gato* and me, we play the game you call chicken. *El muy valiente gato, no?*" Pablo laughed and gunned the motor.

Mooshie glanced up from licking his nonexistent *testículos* and gave Pablo a Clint Eastwood squint that translated as, *Make my day, hombre.*

Pablo returned Mooshie's stare, one eyebrow raised. Mooshie went back to licking. Before I could scream, the truck shot forward and ran over my cat. In that split second of terror-stricken panic, all I saw was Pablo's rear bumper flash and disappear.

My eyes jerked back to the spot where Mooshie had been—and still was—licking between his back toes, and paring his claws with his teeth, totally unconcerned. There wasn't so much as a drop of motor oil on him.

The following evening Mooshie didn't show up for dinner or his nighttime massage. I was just beginning to get nervous when the phone rang.

"Hello" never made it off my tongue, which was just as well since the blaring Mariachi music and high-pitched shouts of ieyiiii ieyiiii would have drowned me out.

"*Hola, Señora!*" screamed Pablo. "It is Pablo calling you."

My mind jumped to the worst-case scenario: Pablo was going to tell me that *El muy valiente gato* had lost the chicken game and was now *pollo muerto*. I began hyperventilating—not that Pablo was paying attention, for he was laughing and yelling rapid-fire Spanish at the top of his lungs to someone named Gordito.

Pablo must have picked up on my apprehension. "Do not worry. *El Gato* is here. He *es mi amigo, mi familia, mi hermano!*" A great roar of cheers and whistles drowned out his next few words, but I had a vision of Mooshie sitting atop a piñata, batting at the stick as it swung by.

"Pablo, are you drunk? And why is *El Gato* with you?"

"*Sí, Señora,* I am very drunk, but we have a fiesta for *El Gato*. He hides in my truck while I work. When I get home*, ay caramba! El Gato* jump out. He eat more guacamole and tortillas than even Gordito! My girlfriend, she say she no love me no more. She say she love *El Gato!* But don't worry, *Señora*. I bring him back to you tomorrow morning."

There was another roar from the crowd.

"What is my cat doing, Pablo? Why is everyone laughing?"

"*El Gato* is drinking tequila, and he is dancing!"

I groaned, desperately trying to ignore the images of my alcoholic cat doing the Mexican Hat Dance.

As promised, a repentant and hungover Pablo returned

Mooshie early the next morning. When I examined my cat for wear and tear, I found his underbelly and whiskers caked with dried guacamole. He weighed a full pound more than the week before.

After the Pablo incident I developed a slight concern that Mooshie might get the idea that hiding in strange vehicles always led to fun-filled adventures. That concern was realized the evening I answered the phone to the sound of giggling.

Thinking it was a prank call, I was about to hang up when I heard a woman ask in a heavy southern accent if I was acquainted with a "certain Mushu Pork."

I groaned. "Oh no. Where is he now?"

"Well, right now this sweet thang is sittin' on top of my dinin' room table waitin' on a nip of my wine." There was another salvo of giggles. "Hey, y'all. I'm Pam, the Avon supplier for your area? I was down in Mill Valley today and I reckon this here sweet varmint stowed away in my trunk while I was makin' a delivery.

"I heard some screamin' while I was drivin', but I thought it was my radiator belt. I opened my trunk to get my product case out when I got home, but before I could grab it, this darlin' thang came outta the dark and climbed right up on my shoulder. Scared the crap right outta me. I was so shook up I poured myself a big ol' glass of wine. And do you know what this funny face did?"

"Let me guess. He offered to leave you a sip after he was done?"

"No ma'am. He up and helped hisself. Stuck his whole

darn head right inside that glass and had hisself a snort!"

I waited for the giggling to die down and checked my watch. I had forty minutes before I was to meet Nice Boyfriend for dinner. "Where are you? I'll pick him up."

"Well, bless your heart, but I'm all the way up here in Sacramento. Don't you worry none; I'm fixin' to come on down with my Friday delivery. I don't mind holdin' onto this here sugar plum, 'cause well, I'm a new divorcée (*day-vor-say*) and I don't like drinkin' alone."

This time my cat was returned to me smelling like the perfume counters at Macy's during Christmas. Attached to his collar were no less than six sparkly pink bows. His nails (front *and* back) were each painted in a different shade of pink.

Sitting him down in front of a mirror so he could see how ridiculous he looked, I explained about the dangers of taking rides from strangers. I told him why he needed to wise up and realize once and for all that there was, in Dorothy's words, no place like home.

Sigh. No such luck.

*

Natalie, the Right Bank's newest and most mysterious tenant, was an attractive fortyish woman who moved into Right Bank Cottage #2 with three small boxes and a suitcase. As far as any of us could tell, she never once opened her blinds, never spoke to anyone, and never turned on a light. None of us ever witnessed her entering or leaving her cottage. After a few months I grew so concerned I would tiptoe to her cottage each night and sniff around the door for the smell of a decomposing body.

One Sunday in early November, I was stacking firewood on the porch when a shiny Lincoln town car with deeply tinted windows slowly rolled into the parking lot and stopped. Mooshie and I waited, but when no one got out, I went back to my stacking.

Mooshie, suffering from another flare-up of his Curiosity-Killed-the-Cat disorder, approached the vehicle to check out the tires, bumpers, and undercarriage. Unable to grasp the concept of respecting boundaries, he vaulted onto the hood to get a closer look at the captain of the ship. He pressed his nose against the windshield. The driver's door flew open and a stately man dressed in a beige suit, black shirt, and cream felt fedora jumped out with surprising agility. He waved his arms and, in a booming bass voice, told Mooshie that the hood of his car was no place for kitty-cats.

He put my cat on the blacktop, but Mooshie was having none of that. He instantly jumped onto the man's shoulder, slid his foreleg around the man's neck, and began passionately licking his hair with obvious jubilation. The man went rigid for a few seconds, then took a pink handkerchief from his breast pocket and busied himself with wiping away Mooshie's dusty pawprints from the hood's spotless black finish—all while my cat continued grooming his hair.

An apology at the ready, I dropped the log I was holding and headed for Mooshie. Before I'd gone two steps, Natalie exited her cottage tricked out in an exquisite black wool suit circa 1945, red gloves, black stockings, sexy red lace-up espadrilles, and a red pillbox hat that was bursting with long black feathers.

She picked my cat off the man's neck and rubbed Mooshie's belly while he made wild attempts to snag her feathers. Lowering him to the ground, she shooed him away, got into the car, and the couple drove off.

This scene would repeat itself from time to time over the next two months, the only difference being that the driver's attitude in respect to my cat had changed dramatically. He began allowing Mooshie to sit on his dashboard while he sang gospel hymns. Mooshie sat perfectly still for each song, as mesmerized by the man's beautiful bass voice as I was.

Who could have predicted that these innocent rendezvous and lovely serenades would lead my cat to abandon his quasi-normal home to become a Baptist?

*

Mooshie began disappearing every Sunday. Without fail he would return in the early evening in better shape than when he left. His coat shined as though it had been brushed repeatedly, and he was putting on weight despite the fact he never touched his food. He often came home smelling of perfume. I was sure he was paying court to several elderly women in the neighborhood who were treating him like the emperor he believed he was.

This went on for a few weeks until the Sunday he didn't return. When he still hadn't returned by Monday, I was in full panic mode or FPM for short. I organized a dragnet, nailed up posters, and called the local SPCA and Animal Control every two hours.

I waited by the phone while Simon canvassed the neighborhood, knocking on doors and tacking up posters on every available public space. On Tuesday evening I got a call from a man who introduced himself as Mr. Walker, pastor of a Baptist church in a town not far from Mill Valley. He went on to inform me that my cat was presently in his church.

Twenty minutes later I was searching for a place to park in the church lot. It wasn't easy; the lot was packed. I managed to squeeze the Chevy into a tight space between a statue of an angel blowing a horn and an iron fence. Before I even stepped out of the car, I could hear the choir singing a joyous tune, their blended voices echoing off the surrounding buildings.

Rounding the corner to the front of the church I stopped short. The driver of the Lincoln town car stood by the front door greeting parishioners. His spiffy suit had been replaced by somber clergy robes. At his side, wearing her red pillbox hat, was our mysterious Right Bank neighbor, Natalie.

Upon seeing me, Pastor Walker's expression changed from lighthearted to grave. Solemn as a funeral director, he shook my hand. "Welcome to our Tuesday evening gospel choir practice, sister. We would like to talk with you about your cat."

I tensed as my mind played video footage of Mooshie ripping apart the backseat of the Lincoln town car.

"Um, is he okay? Has he done something to your car? I have insurance, so if he's—"

Natalie took hold of my arm. "It's nothing like that. We'd like to show you something we think you'll appreciate."

The pastor took my other arm and together they ushered me into the church where the choir was singing a spirited gospel tune while others in the congregation clapped along.

For a minute I thought they'd invited me there to enlist me in the choir, though using my cat to get me there seemed a desperate measure for recruiting members. I was thinking of a way to politely extricate myself when I was taken aback by the sight of Mooshie lounging on the pulpit ledge looking quite pleased with himself.

"Hey! That's my cat!"

The music and clapping trailed off as Pastor Walker leaned back on his heels. For such a large man, I was impressed with his ability to balance.

"Yes sister, and he is the reason we have invited you here today."

There was a smattering of murmurs among the congregation.

The pastor leaned in and spoke in a confidential tone. "Brother Little King—that's the baptismal name we bestowed upon this fine animal—has become a deeply beloved member of this church over the last few weeks." He clasped his hands and looked up to the heavens as if preparing himself for a sermon. "The first time Brother Little King sought refuge in my car, he—"

"Hold on a minute!" I looked from the pastor to Natalie, then to Mooshie. "You *baptized* my cat?"

Pastor Walker gauged my shocked expression and, realizing that it wasn't a *happy* shocked expression, patted me on the back. "Well now, when I say he was given a baptismal name, I mean baptized in the strictly unsanctioned sense of the word. You see, a few weeks ago while I was waiting on Sister Natalie, Brother Lit—ah, I mean, your cat—slipped into the town car and hid under the backseat. Upon our arrival at the church, he went directly to the pulpit and climbed to the very place you see him now."

I glanced at my cat, who was busy holding court with the minions fussing over him. Before I could explain that all cats gravitated to high places so they could feed their egos by looking down on everyone else, the pastor continued.

"Of course we always returned him to your parking lot after the services. We tried to discourage him, but each Sunday he'd slip into the car and hide until we arrived at the church."

Pastor Walker pressed a hand to his heart. "If you could know the joy he brings to our hearts, you would know what a blessed soul he is! Each time I look into his eyes, I can see he is filled with the Lord's spirit."

I was opening my mouth to say my cat was filled to the brim with something, but it sure as hell wasn't the Lord's spirit when Pastor Walker pressed on.

"All living things on this earth, from the humblest ant to the tallest tree, are God's work, and it is through Him that we are all connected. This is a belief we impart to every member of our congregation no matter how young or old."

He waved a hand in Mooshie's direction. "During the

sermons, this precious animal sits quietly on the pulpit and listens to every word of the Gospel. His presence is a reminder to us all that even the smallest creatures on Earth feel the presence of our Lord's love." Here, the pastor broke into a wide grin. "Why, Brother Little King even partakes of the communion wine!"

Giggling broke out among several members of the assembly.

The sight of my cat on the pulpit surrounded by his worshippers jarred an unexpected memory of a friend who once plotted out Mooshie's astrological chart. Much to my amusement, the chart indicated he was best suited for a career as a religious leader. Ever since then, I occasionally called him Reverend Pancakes; a name he refused to acknowledge. Taking in the scene around me, I temporarily suspended my skepticism about the validity of horoscopes.

The pastor brought up a hand in affirmation. "As the Lord is my witness, I had every intention of returning him to his parking lot after last Sunday's service, but he was not to be found. I'm afraid one of our younger members could not resist temptation and brought Brother Little King home with her."

He peered over the top of his glasses and gave one little girl in a frilly pink dress a reprimanding raise of his eyebrow.

I glanced uncertainly at the phony Holy Roller feline, then back at the pastor, sure that there was a hidden camera hoax going on. Except it wasn't April Fools' Day and *Candid Camera* had been off the air for quite a while. I shook my head in disbelief, sure that I was going to wake up from this crazy dream any minute.

Natalie took my hand. "I know this is an unusual request, but we're asking if you would allow your cat to spend a day or two a week with us. Pastor Walker and the congregation would love to have Brother Little King for our official church cat, and I promise when he is with us he will be well taken care of."

I shifted my gaze to the congregation, who were all grinning like proud new mothers.

"Did someone pay you to do this?" I asked, trying to decide which of my extreme practical joker friends had gone to the trouble of putting this elaborate hoax together.

Mooshie jumped down from his pulpit, climbed up Pastor Walker's robe, hooked his paws around the man's neck, looked directly at me, and took on an imperious expression that could only be interpreted as, *Sinner, from now on you may address me as Your Holiness*. He then took up grooming the pastor's hair.

Prying Mooshie's claws from Pastor Walker's robes, I hugged the sanctimonious little beast to my chest; not in a tender, fond way, but in more of a just-wait-until-I-get-you-home way.

Risking a riot, I turned to address the pastor and his congregation, trying not to look directly at all those smiling, hopeful faces. "I am sorry, but Brother Little"— I shook my head—"Mooshie is a Buddhist, so you'll just have to unbaptize him."

Their looks of disappointment pelted me like stones,

and the collective groans of dismay instantly made me feel lower than a snail's belly. Any resolve I had about playing the tough love card was sabotaged when the little girl who brought Mooshie home with her hid her face in her mother's skirt and burst into tears. I knew that if I didn't make concessions, the look of misery on that child's face would haunt me to my grave.

"Okay, okay," I sighed. "I'll make a deal with you. You can borrow my cat on Sundays as long as Natalie delivers him back to me before midnight—that's when he turns into a werewolf."

A deep silence fell over the congregation.

I started to explain that I was only kidding when there erupted resounding laughter, then cheers.

On the way home, while I ranted about family loyalty and not making people worry about him, Mooshie sat in the passenger seat staring straight ahead like a surly and unrepentant teenager.

"I'm telling you for the last time, you have to stop doing things like this," I said to no response.

By the time we pulled into the parking lot, my rant had hardened into an iron resolve: No more sleepless nights spent panicking, no more vet bills, drunken fiestas, or southern belles—my wayward cat was going back on the hook whether he liked it or not.

*

Attached to Natalie's Right Bank cottage #2 was Right Bank cottage #2 ½, a small two-room living space occupied by a rather cantankerous elderly woman named Mrs. W, and her white cat, Mr. Snickers.

When I moved into my cottage, Mrs. W vehemently disliked me on sight. I never could figure out what her reasons were for feeling this way, but no matter how nice I was to her, or how many tomatoes and zucchini I gave her from my garden, her low opinion of me never changed.

Normally this would have hurt my feelings, but due to her petite stature (4'11"), and her high-pitched barking voice, each time she'd bare her dentures and yell at me to get out of her sight, I couldn't help but imagine a ferocious barking Chihuahua with false teeth. This vision of her never failed to render me slap-silly with laughter.

I am a person who believes that cats understand what you are saying to them, and the only reason they don't answer back is that they don't care. So naturally, whenever I see a cat I always greet them and try to draw them into a conversation: *Hey there, sweetheart. What beautiful markings you have! Get any new toys lately? Still working on your spraying issues?*

As bad luck would have it, my patio gate and garden patch were only a couple of yards from Mrs. W's front door, where Mr. Snickers liked to sit. Thus it was that every time I worked in my garden or left my patio gate open, I'd automatically fall into a one-sided conversation with him.

If Mrs. W overheard me, she would storm out her door, grab Mr. Snickers then work herself into a lather, threatening to call the police should I ever touch, talk to, or look at her cat again.

With Mooshie's arrival to the Left Bank, the old lady

flipped her lid, barking that my cat was not to associate with her Mr. Snickers because Mooshie was a "damned foreigner cat" and thus a bad influence.

Not long after he was returned to cat-on-a-rope status, Mooshie came into the kitchen one afternoon, his leash dragging behind him. This caught my attention. When he was on the leash, he generally wanted to be as far from the cottage as his line would reach.

Before I could pick him up, he jumped into my arms with a complaining chirp and clung to me. I cooed, petted, and kissed him until he calmed down. I then carried him outside and urged him to go play while he had the chance.

My cat reappeared five minutes later and the scene in the kitchen was replayed, except this time, his heart was racing, and his pupils were fully dilated. He voiced a series of insistent meows that got louder after I'd carried him outside and swung open the gate.

That's when I smelled the smoke.

Stepping onto the narrow path that divided the Left and Right Banks, I saw clouds of smoke billowing through Mrs. W's screen door. Without bothering to knock, I stepped into a small galley-type kitchen and narrowly avoided colliding with Mr. Snickers, who barreled past me and out the door.

The smoke was thick enough that I couldn't see but a few feet ahead. Somewhere beyond the kitchen I heard Mrs. W calling for Mr. Snickers. I followed the sound of her voice and found her kneeling at the side of a bed, one hand lifting the bed skirt and the other holding a lighted candle. The top of the bed and the wall were engulfed in flames.

I shouted over the roar of the fire that she had to get out, but she motioned me away and went back to searching for Mr. Snickers as if there weren't an inferno going on inches from her head. Thinking that she was suffering from a lack of oxygen to the brain, I pulled her to her feet and headed for the kitchen door. She reacted by kicking my shin and pulling out of my grip.

This time I seized her by the arms and dragged her, literally kicking and screaming, out the door.

I yelled for Joni to call the fire department stat and turned back to the old woman—who was not where I left her. I darted back into #2 ½. The smoke was now pitch black. Blindly inching my way into the main room, I stumbled over Mrs. W who was crawling toward the wall of flames that had been her bedroom.

Fueled by a surge of adrenaline, I held my breath, picked the woman up, and turned in the direction of the only exit—the kitchen door. The kitchen, which shared a common wall with the bedroom, was also in flames. Unable to see for the black smoke, I made a headlong dash in the direction of the kitchen door.

The instant my foot hit the outside doormat, I felt a slight tug at my back and heard a loud popping sound that propelled me and Mrs. W into the yard. The explosion that immediately followed sent the screen door flying off its hinges, trailed by a ball of flame.

Later, I would learn that the gas stove, situated next to

the kitchen door, had exploded. For months afterward, I would have nightmares about what would have happened had I reached that door one second later.

After the fire department left and Mrs. W's niece had been called to pick her up, Joni and I sat with the old woman to wait. We tried to reassure her that once Mr. Snickers came out of hiding we'd make sure he was taken care of until he could be reunited with her.

Mrs. W was not to be solaced. Arms tightly crossed over her birdlike chest she told me in that high barky voice that the fire had been all my fault and that if I hadn't interfered, everything would be fine. She then told Joni that I'd been plotting to steal Mr. Snickers for years.

I don't know for sure what set me off. Maybe it was the voice or the old lady's mulishness—whatever it was, I bolted, burying my face in my sweatshirt to muffle my snorts of wheezy laughter.

An hour later, after Mrs. W had been whisked away, Lindo arrived. Joni and I related the chain of events while he took measure of the burned cottage. By the time we'd each had a turn at inspecting the inside of the charred building, it was time to start dinner.

Upon opening my patio gate, I was greeted by the sight of Mooshie and Mr. Snickers peacefully curled up next to one another. Despite the chaotic events that had taken place just fifteen feet away, both felines were serenely blissed-out—perfect examples of the Zen nature of cats.

· 9 ·
BELLING THE CAT

"BEWARE! THE MONKEYS BITE!"
— A street sign in Kathmandu

Despite the Zen nature of cats, to say that Mooshie resented being leashed again is an understatement. He despised the leash as only a feline can. He was full of revenge—an eye for an eye, a claw for a claw, but especially, a tooth for a tooth.

For the first few months that Mooshie was back on his leash, he pushed all my buttons, including, but not limited to: peeing and pooping outside his litterbox, stealing food off the kitchen table, and, waiting until I got home from work to use the litterbox, thus infusing the house with his specialty fragrance.

Every time I came into a room where he was resting, he'd glance up and fix me with a hard stare—the feline version of Michael Corleone's kiss of death. He broke all the rules, tackling the neighbors' feet and legs, ripping up the furniture, and worst of all, starting his own feline branch of Meals on Wheels, a.k.a. Meals on Wings. In six weeks, he'd killed a finch, a hummingbird, and two sparrows. With each kill he would somehow sneak the bloodied corpse into the house and leave it on my pillow. This was not about leaving gifts of gratitude—it was the feline equivalent of the severed horse head scene in *The Godfather.*

I purchased a dozen cotton mice the same size and color as real mice, hoping Mooshie might take out some of his frustration on them. Stubborn to the end, he refused to be appeased. There was no playfully throwing the toys into the air and batting them around. Instead, Mooshie would methodically gut the play mice one at a time until they were unrecognizable. I'd find their little red felt tongues and leather tails deliberately placed where I'd see them—my keyboard, the sink, my pillow.

To give the birds fair warning, I purchased a cat collar with two jingly bells attached. Mooshie's fury knew no bounds. The way he writhed trying to get the noisy things off his neck was like watching an episode of *Exorcist III: The Family Cat.*

At a hundred and fifty dollars for a fifty-minute consultation, bringing him to a cat psychologist was out of the question.

Thinking back on it now, I should have spent the money.

*

I distinctly remember the day Mooshie snapped. I was wearing a sweatshirt imprinted with the architectural specifications of the Golden Gate Bridge, a pair of Bermuda shorts, and flip flops. I'd had a miserable few hours working on a key scene, and as a result, a migraine was looming on my brain's horizon.

I'd just shut down the computer when I happened to glance out the window and caught a glimpse of Mooshie running low to the ground with something in his mouth. He turned toward the front of the house and disappeared.

Racing to intercept him before he could get inside, we faced off on the porch steps, the dead sparrow still clenched in his jaws.

I pulled the dead bird from his mouth, looked my cat in the eye, and yelled, "NO! NO! NO!"

From deep inside Mooshie's brain a biological memory of his prehistoric ancestors surfaced—the saber-toothed tiger, or perhaps, in this case, the Tyrannosaurus rex. His eyes went black and hard and he bared his teeth. It was like watching a time-lapse of the Kraken emerging from the depths of Hell.

Faster than my eyes could see, he sank his teeth into my foot and then my ankle while his claws tore at the flesh of my lower leg. The attack could not have lasted more than two seconds, but it felt like I'd been savaged by a wild beast. I stared open-mouthed at my injuries, unable to grasp what had just happened.

I snatched up the hellbeast, released his harness from the leash, and slid him down the hallway on his butt in the

same way a bowler throws the ball. Mooshie sailed
smoothly into the living room before hooking the back of
the couch like an aircraft's tailhook catching the arresting
wires. He must have thought this was a fight-to-the-death
event because the last thing I saw before I slammed the
door shut was my cat running at me full steam ahead.

Bleeding, I marched down to Joni's cottage, feeling
slightly muddled and strangely disconnected from my body.
Why were my feet and legs going numb? Should I call the
vet or go to the ER first? All these questions would soon
be laid to rest owing to the fact that as I pressed Joni's
doorbell, I sank to my knees and passed out cold.

The ER doctor who tended to my wounds did not
believe it was a small domestic cat that had done the
damage.

"It's a good thing you trapped the animal," he said.
"You'll need to contact Animal Control—they'll visit the
owner to make sure the animal has had its rabies shots and
is kept under lock and key."

Somewhat abashed, I cleared my throat. "Ah, actually,
"the animal" has had all his vaccinations. He belongs to me.
I scolded him for killing a bird, but I think I caught him at
a bad time."

The doctor raised his eyebrows. "You caught your cat at
a bad time? Was he late for a meeting or something?" He
got up to leave. "I'd hate to see what he would have done
if he'd been seriously pissed off."

He came back a few minutes later and handed me a piece
of paper. "This is a document for Animal Control promising

that you'll keep your small ferocious savage quarantined for a full ten days. You'll have to sign it." He chuckled and added, "If your beast has another bad day, we can't have him terrorizing the neighborhood."

I found Joni waiting in the lobby. On the drive home, she told me as tactfully as she could that she might have taken Mooshie in for the duration of his quarantine, but she was raising two new kittens and didn't want to take the chance that he'd go psycho again.

Things were mighty chilly around my house for those next ten days. My cat and I did not speak, nor did we eat together. We slept in different rooms, and if I happened to touch him, he would dart out of my reach and remove all traces of contact by frantically licking away the contamination. What I found particularly unsettling was that this was roughly the same pattern that each of my ex-boyfriends followed right before breaking up with me.

That my cat was dumping me was sad, but that I'd been the victim of domestic abuse at the claws and teeth of my cat was downright demoralizing. I doubted things could get any worse. Within an astonishingly short time I was to discover what a faulty notion that was.

Mooshie and I were still not speaking when the rent on our cottage was raised again, with promises of regular future raises. I did the math and realized that my combined salaries as a nurse and an author would not keep up with the skyrocketing rate of inflation in Marin, which was fast becoming a haven for the rich and famous.

The deadline for *Mercy* was hanging over me like the

sword of Damocles. I've never done well with deadlines, and my intermittent spells of writer's block were making me a nervous wreck. Everything I wrote came out sounding like "My Summer Vacation" as written by a first grader zoned out on Ritalin.

Added to all that, understaffing at the hospital was a growing concern for both the nurses and our patients. It was our licenses on the line, and our patients' safety that was at risk.

And the *coup de grâce*? Nice Boyfriend began dropping broad hints that it was time for us to move on—in different directions.

Much to my relief, Mooshie sensed my despair and returned to his old sleeping quarters on the pillow next to mine—and not a night too soon.

*

I was pulled to consciousness from a dream in which I was being choked by a fur scarf. Opening my eyes, I found Mooshie sitting on my neck like an eight-pound goiter. He stared at me, his ears perked stiffly forward.

I stared back.

He lowered his head, and deliberately bit the end of my nose.

From the corner of my eye, the bedside clock glowed a bright blue 3:01 a.m.

I was scheduled to appear on CNN later that morning to discuss the politics of healthcare, so I chose to turn a deaf ear to whatever Mooshie was trying to tell me. I closed my eyes and willed myself to drift back to sleep.

The odor of alcohol dragged me back to full consciousness. I was sure I'd locked the kitchen cabinet that held the dry sherry and I doubted my cat would be desperate enough to drink the rubbing alcohol.

Mooshie head-butted my nose then licked my left eyelid open.

The rebuke I was about to utter froze on my tongue. Someone was jingling keys close by. More perturbing, they sounded like *my* keys.

I shifted my gaze past Mooshie to the end of the bed. In the dim light given off by the small flashlight he held between his teeth, a stranger was busy rifling through my purse.

The situation was so unreal, I remained calm. Or maybe it was Mooshie's comforting presence that lulled me into a false sense of security. I snorted and shifted my legs to give the impression I was waking from a deep sleep.

The man went still and switched off the flashlight.

I waited a few seconds then faked steady soft snores until he slipped into the hall. Mooshie moved as if to follow the burglar, but I grabbed his back legs and pushed him under the covers.

A hundred thoughts sprang to mind like a mob of panicked kangaroos. Dialing 911 was out of the question—the burglar would be sure to hear me and what if he had a gun? I had nothing within reach that could be used to defend myself except a blue princess phone and a ceramic cat lamp.

I concluded that apart from our lives, my computer, and the envelope containing Jerry Garcia's fingernail clippings and a lock of his hair, the contents of our house were mostly future donations to Goodwill. The happy thought that I might never have to have another garage sale was crossing my mind when the thief moved into my office and opened the file cabinet.

I did some quick calculating as I slipped noiselessly out of bed. The trespasser was an unknown and drunk, possibly out of his mind on drugs as well. While I didn't care what he burgled, I *did* care that the next room he would undoubtedly enter was the one in which Simon was sleeping.

I envisioned what might happen were Simon to awaken to the sight of some drunk walking off with his custom-built skateboard—there would be a struggle, then a gun suddenly appearing, and—

I broke into a cold sweat. Behind me, Mooshie chirped. The intruder passed my room, and to my relief, went into the bathroom where I heard the telltale squeak of the medicine cabinet door. I doubted that the four bottles of Mylanta and the jar of Vicks VapoRub would hold his interest for very long.

Right or wrong, I made the choice to deal with the situation head-on. With a sigh and a prayer, I walked into the hall and flipped on the lights.

A barefoot man wearing a garish zebra-striped tank top stepped out of the bathroom. His head was shaved and there was a multicolored tattoo of a snake winding from one pierced ear, around his neck, and down the length of his arm. Of one thing I was sure—he would not be difficult to identify in a police lineup.

I couldn't help but notice he was gaping at me, a bemused expression on his face. I glanced at the reflection in the hall mirror and considered the woman dressed in red droopy long johns equipped with a butt flap. Her teeth were covered by an unsightly tooth guard and her hair was rolled around an assortment of tomato paste and frozen orange juice cans. Admittedly, I resembled a circus clown attempting to contact aliens via a homemade antenna system.

Taking advantage of the thief's momentary distraction, I rushed him, pushing him away from Simon's room and into the living room. To make things even more surreal, the guy started laughing. I'm not sure what he found so amusing, but his glee quickly turned to something dark. His eyes went hard and his expression could only be interpreted as the fun was over and it was time to do some harm.

I instantly resorted to screeching like a banshee.

Simon, fuzzy from sleep, came out of his room, took in the scene before him, and, thinking it was all part of some wild dream, started back to bed. I shouted that he wasn't dreaming and to call 911. Like a pinball, he changed direction and headed for the phone.

This had a sobering effect on our intruder. In one swift move he grabbed Simon and dragged him to the back door. The thug may have been smooth with the combat moves, but he was clueless about the lengths a mother will go to protect her child. He also knew nothing about Mooshie's Bite and Chase game or the dangers of going barefoot in our house.

Before the miscreant went another step, Mooshie clamped his front claws into the guy's left calf muscle while shredding the top of his foot with his hind claws. Cursing, the thief tried shaking him off, which was Mooshie's cue to take the Bite and Chase game to the rough rodeo level. Without further encouragement, my cat dug in and sank his teeth into the man's inner thigh.

I counted on Mooshie riding it out as I jammed my knee into the thief's groin. In perfect synchronicity, Simon slammed an elbow into his ribs. The group effort drove the man out onto the patio. Before fleeing into the night, the burglar dislodged Mooshie with a kick that launched him to the other side of the living room.

After the police were gone and Simon had returned to bed, I brewed a pot of tea. Sitting with Mooshie over our tea and toast, I made up my mind—I wanted a divorce from status quo and normal.

*

Over the next six months, I wandered around the nooks and crannies of my life, thinking about how I might make room for change and growth. I wanted to break out of the safe little box I'd built around my life. The time was right— I'd finished *Mercy* and sent it to the publisher, so I had the luxury of having more free time.

Perhaps it was the memory of the green flash, or maybe it was just a need to get away, but the pull of Montserrat was irresistible. I went back to the island for a second visit, staying in the same house I occupied the first time I'd been to the island. Through my Montserratian and expatriate friends I learned that the owners of the house were searching for a new caretaker.

Before leaving for California, I contacted them in London and offered my services as a live-in caretaker—gratis. They were more than happy to accept.

Three months later I gave up the cottage I'd rented for eighteen years, sold my '57 Chevy, returned the bulk of my belongings to Goodwill, and bid adieux to my friends. Simon, excited about my upcoming adventure, moved in full time with his dad.

The irreplaceable, essential things that made up my life—my computer containing my life's work, my skills as a critical care nurse, and my cat—went with me to the Emerald Isle of the Caribbean.

PART THREE

MUSHU PORK WITH PANCAKES—TO GO

· 10 ·

THE TRAVELING CIRCUS
COMES TO TOWN

"My objective in examining the Egyptian cat mummy was to find signs of evolutionary transformation. Anatomically speaking, I found no differences whatsoever—the three-thousand-year-old cat was completely indistinguishable from a Parisian alley cat of today."
— Georges Cuvier, French naturalist (1769 -1832)

There is a consensus among cat fanciers that Burmese are the most affectionate of cat breeds. They also agree on the standard of Burmese physical traits: prominent gold, yellow, or green eyes, a short muzzle and rounded head, and a compact and muscular body—like a brick wrapped in silk.

Where opinions begin to diverge is on how well Burmese cats take to travel. Opinions ran the gamut from

Best Traveler in Show, to Homebody. British breeders tend to think one can send Burmese cats to the moon and they'll enjoy every minute of the trip, then beg for a flight to Mars. American breeders believe Burmese don't take to travel one bit and if they are forced to travel outside a five-block radius of their nests, they will perish on the spot.

Before we began our nomadic life, I believed in the British version of Burmese as traveling fanatics. As I was soon to discover, Mooshie subscribed to the American belief that travel is an unnatural and terrifying state. Knowing how firmly he was set in his ways, it is surprising that he adapted as well as he did to the next phase of our lives—not that he had a choice.

Having no desire to traumatize my cat any more than necessary on his maiden voyage into the world, I thought it best if we made our way to the Caribbean slowly, stepping-stone style. Our first scheduled stop was the Southern California home of my down-to-earth friend, Janey. I rented a car and outfitted it with everything a spoiled cat might need for his trip—litterbox, toys, ground turkey and chicken gizzards, English Breakfast tea, travel carrier, and water.

Mooshie was fine as we drove through Mill Valley at a steady thirty miles per hour. He languidly stretched, then arranged his body across the top of the backseat and commenced grooming. I was so ecstatic over how well my cat traveled that I began fantasizing about all the wonderful places he and I would explore. Visions of my cat tucked into a front-facing papoose while we took in the wonders of the Grand

Canyon and the quaint towns of New England danced through my head.

That fantasy lasted until I drove onto the entrance ramp of Highway 101 and hit forty-two miles per hour. Heart-wrenching wails sounded from the backseat. Certain Mooshie was in his death throes, I pulled off at Sausalito to check him over.

The fur along the ridge of his back was up and his pupils were fully dilated. I moved him to the front seat, thinking he might feel better draped around my neck or on the dashboard.

He wouldn't go near the dash, but he did calm down after settling himself in my lap—until I hit fifty-five miles per hour and the yowling resumed. It made no difference whether I was driving at fifty-five or seventy-five miles per hour, just as it didn't matter if he was in or out of his travel cage, on my lap, over my shoulders, or under the seat—for the seven-hour, 450-mile trip to Corona del Mar, his cries of protest went on without surcease. For a cat who always had such a passionate desire to be inside, under, or on cars, his extreme discomfort at traveling in one was baffling.

I entered Janey's house complaining bitterly about the nerve-wracking ordeal my cat put me through. Janey, who was cuddling a now perfectly relaxed and purring Mooshie, looked skeptical.

Somewhere in the twenty feet between the car and the house, my cat had metamorphosed from a victim of torture-by-automobile into a charming houseguest.

*

Janey and her husband owned two dogs. One was an elderly, mentally addled, blind, and stone-deaf mongrel they called Rastamon. The other was the undisciplined and out-of-control golden retriever aptly named The Great Saphenous. Bearing in mind that these two were Mooshie's first up-close-and-personal canines, my cat astonished me with his Buddha-like attitude toward them.

The first time Rastamon stumbled into our room sniffing and bumping his way around (think Mr. Magoo), Mooshie watched him intently, his expression a mixture of curiosity and pity for the aged. When Rastamon walked into him, Mooshie didn't run or hiss. Instead, he placed his paw squarely between Rastamon's eyes and held him at foreleg's length.

The mutt, sensing a resisting object, turned and exited the room.

Saphenous was an altogether different story. The morning after we arrived, I brought Mooshie upstairs in his travel carrier, intending to let him hang out with me and Janey on the deck. The carrier no sooner touched the floor than Saphenous came bounding from the house and, without so much as a howdy-do, fell upon the plastic box with unrestrained zeal. The next three minutes were a free-for-all as Janey and I tried to get the carrier away from the crazed canine.

Despite our efforts, Saphenous succeeded in getting a tooth-hold on the handle, and half carried, half dragged the loaded carrier to the other end of the house, where he got a start on trying to chew off the clasps. At length, Janey wrested the cage out of Saphenous's mouth and heaved it over to me. I beat a hasty retreat to our room, where I cautiously opened the carrier door.

Mooshie lay on his side purring, none the worse for rough treatment. Once out of his carrier, however, he began a rapid and fastidious post-maul grooming. As he lifted his hind leg to preen his nether parts, the persistent Saphenous threw his weight against our door, knocking it open. Repeating his wild jumping and barking frenzy, the dog set eyes on my cat.

Frozen in place with his hind leg in the air, Mooshie watched the wild dog show wearing a mixed expression of wonder and disgust.

Unable to help himself, Saphenous pranced over and unceremoniously stuck his snout into the very area my cat was grooming.

In a flash Mooshie lowered his leg, clutched the retriever's head between his claws, and sunk his teeth into the top of the dog's forehead.

The canine drama queen squealed and bucked about the room, swinging his head side-to-side in an attempt to dislodge my cat. Mooshie held on like a bronco buster going for the ten-thousand-dollar purse, using all the power in his hind legs to thump the dog's snout.

After a few more seconds of bronco busting, Mooshie jumped clear, pausing only long enough to hiss before he resumed his toilette, licking off any dog slime that might be clinging to his silky fur.

Saphenous stood at a safe distance and regarded my cat

with what I interpreted as shock mixed with admiration. Or, he might have been trying to decide whether or not to take on Mooshie for a second round.

Mooshie paused in his grooming and shot the dog a reproachful look that said, *Plenty more where that came from, pal.*

Saphenous gave voice to a long whine of complaint, punctuated by a sharp bark.

Bored with the dog's need for attention, Mooshie ignored him.

Unused to being shunned, Saphenous looked to me, as if asking for an explanation. Giving the dog a friendly scratch behind the ears, I shook my head and shrugged. "Don't take it personally, Saph. He's a cat, and with cats there are no explanations or answers. It's the way they've always been, and if we're lucky, they'll be that way to the end of time."

*

Janey was the one who got my cat addicted to cat treats. It didn't take much; one or two of these tidbits turned Mooshie into a cat snack addict with a can-a-day habit. These supposedly harmless goodies were addictive enough that I began referring to them as cat smacks. Each time Mooshie indulged himself with the miniature fish, beef, or poultry flavored triangles, he wore the same dazed expression I'd seen on the hardcore heroin addicts who frequented my ER.

The allure of these miniature tidbits was so powerful that a shake of the can would draw his immediate and full attention. Dubious as I was about their nutritional benefits, I'll admit the smack snacks came in handy on more than one occasion.

Janey's house sat on a cliff overlooking the Pacific Ocean. Seeing as how Mooshie would soon be living on a small island in the middle of the Caribbean Sea, I thought it would be a good idea to introduce him to the largest body of water on Earth. I carried him to the beach cove directly below the house, put him on his leash, and let him go. He sniffed at a few odd pieces of driftwood before stretching out on the warm sand, rolling side to side in ecstasy. After a quick lick bath, he turned to watch the ocean waves.

It took about five minutes for his brain to begin processing the reality of what he was actually looking at. Once his brain registered the image and sent it to his reasoning center, his thoughts were made visible in the way his body tensed and his pupils dilated: *Wait a minute—is that . . . water? No, it can't be. But wait. Oh my god, I think it IS water, but . . . but there's so MUCH of it, and it's rolling right for me! I've got to RUN!*

No, no, no . . . wait. It's rolling back! I must have scared it away. Whew, I thought it was going to get me for sure. But . . . it changed its mind! WHOA! It's coming for me again! Run for your life!

Ears laid back, Mooshie went into a crouch so low his belly left a distinct trail in the sand. In a full-tilt boogie zigzag, he headed for the hills.

Confident the leash would hold, I watched him go only slightly ashamed of myself for laughing. I scurried after him, thinking I would calm him with some soothing words and snacks. I wasn't prepared when, like magic, Mooshie Houdini slipped out of his halter and disappeared into one of the small canyons that bordered the beach.

For the remainder of the day and well into the evening, we conducted an all-out Search-and-Rescue operation. We checked with neighbors, posted notices on utility poles, and even sent Saphenous into the canyon, urging him to use his retriever skills to find the wayward feline. An hour later the dog returned carrying an ancient rabbit carcass.

Giving up the search for the night, I lay awake tormented by the thought that Mooshie might have made it up to the busy Pacific Coast Highway. I doubted any animal could survive that roadway. Around two in the morning I went out onto the deck and called softly, mimicking his come-play-with-me call. I absentmindedly shook the cat snacks can while scanning the dark canyon. From the east end of the canyon, I thought I heard a faint *merrow*. I began shaking the can vigorously and made the trilling call that usually grabbed his attention.

Mooshie jumped onto the deck ten minutes later, his fur caked with mud and burrs. He rubbed against my leg and voiced a desperate chirp that let me know just how desperately he missed his smack snacks. I was so relieved he was alive and in one piece, I let him have his way with the whole can.

Three days later, we were scheduled to board a plane for Puerto Rico where I'd arranged to stay at my friend Julie's apartment. At the airline check-in counter, the austere middle-aged clerk scrutinized Mooshie's health certificates.

Whether out of curiosity or duty, the clerk peered through the holes in the carrier. On cue, Mooshie stuck a paw through an air hole, waved, and chirped a happy greeting.

The clerk chuckled and asked if he could take a closer look at "the animal." Never having flown with a cat before, I complied, thinking it was standard operating procedure for airline personnel to check out animal passengers to make sure they were what the documents claimed they were and not some miniaturized hijacker wearing a cat or dog costume.

I held him out to the clerk, who took him somewhat awkwardly. Always happy to make new friends, Mooshie put his arms around the man's neck and began licking off his cologne. I never could figure out if he did this because he liked the taste of cologne and hair pomade, or if he found the smells offensive and wanted to get rid of them.

Making quiet cooing sounds, the clerk stroked Mooshie's head until he noticed the other clerks staring at him. He regained his composure and placed my cat on the counter. Mooshie took in the crowd of humans watching him. Realizing he was on center stage, Mooshie the ham launched into his tried-and-true opening act—he sat up like a meerkat, his front legs hanging at his sides.

Laughter broke out among those in line behind us. Travelers rushing by slowed to get a better look, then continued on, smiles on their faces.

Remaining on his hind legs, he issued a complicated series of chirps and twitters as if he were telling a cat joke. (*A Persian, a Siamese, and a Maine Coon walk into a bar one night . . .*)

Delighted, our fellow travelers applauded the talking cat. I wondered if Mooshie would prove to be a high point of their day. I hoped that when they reached their destinations tired and hungry, a few would recall the amusing airport cat and their spirits would lift.

Whatever it was about animals that softened people's hard edges and made them happy, Mooshie had it in spades.

The reservation clerk issued my cat a paper ticket bearing the name Mr. Mushu Pork and attached it to his carrier. In a deserted corner near the boarding gate, I took him out and settled him on my lap where he could observe the planes on the runway. The thunderstorm that was underway did not distract him from concentrating on the planes ascending and landing. Each time an aircraft flew by, Mooshie crouched and chattered in the same way as when birds came into his line of vision.

My initial theory was that if he was comfortable watching the giant plane-birds in flight, he might not be so fretful being inside of one. That supposition proved to be full of holes when I stowed him under the seat in front of me and his plaintive high-pitched meows came into force.

As the wheels left the tarmac, the volume of his cries increased then morphed into outright caterwauling. I scrunched down and feigned sleep as the passengers around us turned in their seats, searching for the source of the horrible noise.

We were about four hundred feet off the ground when a deafening bang shook the plane. At the same instant, a blue ball of light about fifteen inches in diameter streaked down the aisle to the rear of the plane where it collapsed in on itself and vanished.

Never before had I experienced such profound silence on an aircraft. Even Mooshie's screams for salvation, which were loud enough to be heard over the roar of the jet's engines upon takeoff, abruptly stopped. The silence continued for what seemed like forever until the pilot announced that we'd been hit by lightning but no damage had been done. The blue sphere was never addressed.

Flashback to 1963—my family was gathered at my aunt's cabin on Saratoga Lake when a severe thunderstorm erupted. We were inside playing cards when a similar blue ball of lightning rolled through the room and out the back door, knocking over a floor lamp as it went.

My father, a knowledgeable naturalist and former forester with the United States Forest Service, explained that the rare phenomenon we'd been lucky enough to witness was known as ball lightning. That I'd seen it twice in one lifetime seemed like an omen of eventful adventures to come.

By the time we arrived at Julie's apartment, Mooshie was dehydrated but refused to drink water from the tap. I took an unopened bottle of water from my carry-on and poured half of it into his bowl. He eagerly lapped it up.

A half-hour later the building supervisor came to the door with two gallons of bottled water and the news that the tap water had been contaminated due to a break in the building's water main. From that day forward I would not drink the water any place we went without first testing it out on Mooshie—my very own canary in a coal mine.

During the day, I left Mooshie comfortably asleep in our air-conditioned room and went about the task of procuring a printer, paper, a year's supply of cat food, and dry goods. I also found a cargo pilot who flew supplies to Antigua and Montserrat twice a month in his own plane. Evenings I devoted exclusively to devising a no-fail plan of bringing Mooshie onto Montserrat.

On my previous visits to Montserrat, I noticed an absence of cats. According to the official rules, there were no restrictions on bringing dogs and cats to the island as long as they had their vaccination and health records. Intrigued, I asked around as to the reason why the island was devoid of felines.

According to the Montserratian folk religion, a jumbie is an evil spirit that stands at the heart of numerous superstitions and tales of horror. Jumbies are said to inhabit the bodies of snakes, dead people, and—cats. I was told that this belief accounted for the disappearance of cats brought to the island by British and American expatriates; most of which were, to use the Montserratian vernacular, "stashed."

*

The twin-engine Piper Aztec was old, tired, and in desperate need of repair. The navigation system sometimes malfunctioned and the radio, our only connection to terra firma, was iffy. I was soon to discover that our pilot was, in aviator slang, an "air cowboy." Overconfident in his abilities, he was one of those pilots who turned into a risk-taking twit the moment he was airborne.

On the morning of our departure, I peered into the back of the plane and my jaw dropped. The space that once held the passenger seats was now packed solid with what appeared to be hundreds of pounds of vegetables and frozen meat. Somewhere under the frozen chickens, my supplies were being crushed, and my computer dripped upon. But it wasn't my supplies and computer that concerned me—it was the weight that made me nervous. Besides breaking numerous FAA rules, I doubted the aircraft would even be able to get off the ground.

It was with some trepidation that I belted myself into the co-pilot seat. Thanks to the mild sedative I'd slipped into his breakfast tea, Mooshie slept soundly in his carrier stowed behind my seat.

Groaning and squeaking, the plane cleared the end of the runway by a whisker. The engine straining, we climbed foot by laborious foot to the airspace just below the clouds. In a death-defying ride that lasted for three and a half hours, we bumped and dipped our way over the Caribbean Sea.

Twenty-five miles away from what the pilot thought "might" be Montserrat, (the radio quit ten minutes out of Puerto Rico) he sheepishly informed me that due to his miscalculations of cargo weight, speed, wind resistance, and distance, we were flying on fumes. He then shouted instructions on how to prepare for a water landing: "Crunch down into a ball!" According to the air cowboy, this maneuver afforded me a 30 percent chance of survival.

I've had several panic-inducing plane rides in my time: I've been lost over the Bermuda Triangle during a bad storm with a pilot who'd lost radio contact with the tower, I've choked on smoke pouring into the cabin during an emergency landing, been in a commercial jet when it skidded off the runway upon landing, and, of course, my latest aviation misadventure of being hit by lightning upon takeoff. None of those events were as frightening as being told by a panicking pilot that he'd "miscalculated" the amount of fuel required for the trip, and because of that, we were definitely going down.

So certain was I that we were going to die, I bypassed all levels of panic and went directly to the silent resignation of the doomed. Call it irrationality or blind hope, but at the moment of truth, my only concern was how to prevent my cat from perishing as well. I don't remember thinking in any logical fashion as I ripped off my safety harness and crawled over the boxes of frozen chicken. Squished between the crates and the ceiling, I tore through the supplies, desperate to find something that might save my cat from drowning. I let out the breath I'd been holding when I found a boogie board wedged between the cabin wall and the crates. Using every ounce of strength I had, I pried the board loose and untied two of the ropes that secured the frozen meat crates.

My idea was to lash Mooshie's carrier to the board, then throw it out of the plane at the last minute before we crashed into the sea. As preposterous as this improvised life raft was, if there was even a shred of a chance it would keep my cat afloat long enough to reach the shore, it was worth a try.

I was reaching for Mooshie's carrier when the pilot gave a jubilant shout. Through a gap between the crates, I recognized Chances Peak, the highest point of Montserrat's soon-to-be-famous Soufrière Hills stratovolcano.

The pilot banked sharply for the dicey approach to the runway and barked that I should return to my seat and buckle in. Giddy with relief, I did as I was told. That was when the engines made a klunk-splutter noise and quit. Pale and sweating, the cowboy frantically jockeyed the controls as we glided too far left of the runway over the rocky strip of land that separated the tarmac from the sea. There could not have been twenty feet between the plane and the rocks when by some divine intervention, the plane drifted to the right, safely over the runway.

We touched down and coasted to the small aircraft parking area. If it wasn't for the dead propeller and the silent engine, it might have appeared to the untrained eye to be a perfectly good landing instead of a narrowly missed disaster.

Ten minutes later I was walking across the tarmac holding three fruit flats marked STRAWBERRIES—USA PRODUCE. Although the paperwork stated there was a total of twenty-four pints of strawberries, eight pints to a flat, I was only too aware that the bottom two flats did not hold sixteen pints of strawberries, but rather an eight-pound feline jumbie.

I mentally went over the speech I planned on giving the

Montserratian airport authorities. *"These? They're strawberries for the chef at the hotel. It's strawberry shortcake night."*

I tripped over an iguana sunning on the tarmac and the top flat tipped forward, threatening to fall. Afraid I may have jarred the jumbie awake, I put the flats down and gathered up the few strawberries that had tumbled out of their baskets. Listening carefully, I heard a slight rustling of fur against the cardboard, a grunting snore, then all was quiet.

I picked up the flats and entered the airport, praying to the cat jumbies that be, that I'd calculated everything correctly, from the dosage of the sedative to the amount of time it would take to get through Immigration and Customs.

The dividing line between Montserrat Immigrations and Montserrat Customs was blurry. To the casual observer, they appeared to be a one-stop-shop, ergo, the guy who stamped your passport might also be the same guy who went through your bags.

At that time, visitors were rarely questioned as to why they were there, and as far as I knew nothing was ever confiscated. Other than abiding by international law, I believe the only reason for Customs on the island was to amuse the officials.

The expatriates and tourists provided them with years' worth of tales about the strange fare we all carried in our luggage. On my last visit to the island my electric pedicure tool touched off such a stir, I was asked to demonstrate its use. There was also intense questioning and a disastrous demonstration involving my glue gun, but that's another story and one that may still be told in the streets of Montserrat to this day.

The Montserratian fascination with travelers' strange grooming tools also extended to food items that were not readily available to them. Barbecue-flavored potato chips were coveted, and a jar of Nutella could be used as currency with most of the taxi drivers. Knowing this, I'm not sure why it never occurred to me that most Montserratians had never seen a strawberry, let alone tasted one. Thus, my goodwill gesture of offering the customs officer a few of the luscious berries proved to be a serious miscalculation. Like Costco shoppers at the free sample stands, hands came from every direction with alarming speed, plucking the berries from the baskets. In a few seconds, four of the pint baskets vanished from the top flat.

Once the ventilation slots in the bottom of the flat came into full view, God only knew what my cat would do in his sedated state if he saw hands flying at him from overhead.

It was when the porter's hand landed on one of the four remaining baskets that the customs officer noticed my alarmed expression. Perhaps he mistook it for indignation; more than likely he thought I meant to file a complaint. He told the others that they were not to take any more of the berries. In direct opposition to his own order, he reached in and picked out a few berries for himself.

I felt my cat stir and change position. Alarmed, my eyes went to the ventilation slots where the tiniest bit of Mooshie's fur was sticking through one of the slots. I quickly moved one of the remaining baskets over to cover the slot.

The officer stared at me. "You feelin' okay, sistah? You

lookin' pale. You want me to help you carry dey berries to dey taxi ride?"

"Thank you, but I've got my own ride. I have to hurry and get these berries refrigerated."

Nervous and sounding like a jittery livestock auctioneer, I continued on in this vein, speaking about strawberries growing a furry mold if they got too warm. I threw in words like spirochetes and rickettsia prowazekii bacteria, hoping to lend a note of science to make the excuse more believable.

My blathering came to a halt when I felt Mooshie begin to push his back against the bottom of the top flat. I pounced on him, pushing down the furry spirochete trying to force his way out.

"I've got to go now," I said, moving away from the station. "The chef will not be happy if I let the berries get too furry."

The officer examined the berries in his hand, probably looking for furry mold, and popped one in his mouth. Savoring the flavor, he waved me on.

I made it outside just as one of Mooshie's spindly forelegs shot through a ventilation slot, batting haphazardly, claws extended. I guessed that in the same way sedatives often left patients cranky and hungover, my cat was feeling somewhat cantankerous.

I put my face close to the crate, pretending to examine the berries for damage. "Settle down or you're going to end up as a cat head on a stick instead of the cat on a rope!"

In the parking area, I found the older model Mini Moke,

a small-scale front-drive utility vehicle that my new employers provided for me. After stowing Mooshie's crate safely on the passenger floor, I collected the rest of my luggage and secured it in the cargo area. With a sigh of relief, I headed in the direction of our new home on the other side of the island.

We weren't even clear of the parking lot before Mooshie's angry yowls grew loud enough to rouse every jumbie within a two-mile radius. I pulled over and searched under the passenger seat for the transistor radio my employers said they always kept in the vehicle. Praying the batteries still worked, I clicked it on and found the only station available—a Holy Roller audio wave extravaganza.

Each time we passed through one of the outlying villages, Mooshie's wails would rise to deafening proportion. To drown out my cat's cries for salvation, I turned up the volume on the ranting overzealous preacher.

Startled by the racket, the village residents waved and shouted their spiritual encouragement. I could just imagine the talk that would follow: *"Have you heard? That new white girl who's moving to the north end of the island has found Jesus!"*

Amen!

· II ·

MOOSHIE OF THE JUNGLE

"There are no ordinary cats."
— Colette (1878 – 1954)

The Montserrat house was built for the tropics. Three sides of the building featured an abundance of louvered windows. The fourth side faced the sea, but in place of a wall, there were floor-to-ceiling louvered pocket doors that folded and slid out of sight. This allowed for a breathtaking 180-degree view of the island and the vast Caribbean Sea.

Mooshie was happy living on Montserrat. He was always warm, and despite the land crabs that daily raided his kibble bowl, he ate like a horse. Sleeping under a tent of mosquito netting seemed to provide him with the same sense of security he got when hiding inside cardboard boxes or shopping bags. He was obsessed with roaming the tropical gardens that made up the five-acre estate. I would often find him sitting among the fruit trees, head cocked, ears twitching as he listened intently to the constant cacophony of birds, lizards, frogs, and insects before joining in with a medley of chirps and meows.

Mooshie proved himself to be no fraidy-cat in his new surroundings—except when it came to the agouties and the swimming pool.

The agouti is a rodent that looks like a giant tailless rat that has been bred with a rabbit, a squirrel, and a beaver. Our first encounter with one came a few days after we'd moved in. We were exploring the grounds when we came upon the agouti sitting on his haunches under our banana tree enjoying a bounty of stolen fruit. He was at least eighteen inches long and probably weighed twenty-plus pounds. It didn't surprise me he was so large, considering that at his feet lay the stems and peels of the half dozen bananas he'd already consumed.

Never before having seen anything like him, Mooshie cowered behind me, his fur standing on end. Shy creatures by nature, the agouti dropped the banana and fled, the long fur on his rump bouncing like a woman's flounced skirt.

Mooshie's reaction to the swimming pool was similar to his experience with the Pacific Ocean in that I don't believe he fully understood what it was he was looking at. He demonstrated this lack of conceptualization one afternoon as he lay down on the patio for a nap and a cecropia moth with a six-inch wingspan flew by him. Instantly he was on the chase, leaping and swatting at the thing as it cleverly led him closer to the pool. With a spectacular Baryshnikovian leap, Mooshie grabbed for the moth and splashed down in the pool's deep end.

Let me put to rest the fallacy about cats not being able to swim: cats *do* swim, and quite well, I might add.

Before I could react, he swiftly cat-paddled to the steps at the shallow end and scampered out. He shook himself off, and without so much as a modicum of embarrassment, sauntered to the sun deck where he sat giving the pool careful contemplation. If I didn't know better, I would have said he was thinking about going back in for another dip.

Mooshie was fascinated by the pool, but never so much as the morning we stepped out onto the deck and were struck dumb by the sight before us.

I'd run into iguanas before—in pet shops—but nothing could have prepared me for the six-foot-long, iridescent green and turquoise iguanas sunning themselves along the edges of the pool. Mooshie started chattering and flattened himself to a low crouch, his entire body trembling with anticipation.

The three iguanas took off at the speed of light, heading back into the tropical rainforest. Mooshie raced after them, his lithe body stretched to full length, all four paws off the ground. That split-second image of him, sleek and graceful, took my breath away.

My sense of wonderment over Mooshie's beauty was instantly replaced by the fear I would never see him again. I spent the next hour shaking the smack snack can in various rhythms while blocking out thoughts of Mooshie running into Salem, a sweet machete-wielding, jumbie-hunting Montserratian man who frequently appeared out of nowhere to check on me and the house.

This wrinkle added another difficulty to my search for Mooshie. I couldn't very well go about calling "here kitty, kitty, kitty" for the simple reason any Montserratian passing through the tropical forest would think I was summoning jumbies. Instead, I sang Irish tunes with repeated choruses of "here ditty ditty ditty" and "hoochie-coochie Mooshie" all at top volume, and in an Irish brogue.

My cat pranced onto the veranda a few hours later carrying a dead chameleon. Trailing behind him was an emaciated black and white cat with striking green eyes.

Overjoyed that another feline existed on the ailurophobic island, I squelched the impulse to grab my cat and put him on his leash. Mooshie, looking touchingly proud, ceremoniously set the dead lizard near his companion, then sat back to watch as she hungrily devoured the thing.

In the same haughty manner one might use to summon a waiter with a snap of the fingers, Mooshie turned to me with a curt *brrrpt!*

I took this as a royal command that tuna and fresh water were to be served without delay. I put out two dishes of cat food, a bowl of water, and another of kibbles.

Mooshie sniffed the food bowls, sampled a bite, then called to the refugee. She hurried to the food, watchful as she went. Issuing a few warning growls, she inhaled both bowls of food while Mooshie observed from a non-threatening distance. Done with the good stuff, she sniffed the kibbles, and in a show of cat scorn, attempted to bury them with invisible dirt. She then wandered to the path leading back into the forest.

Before she disappeared from view, Mooshie issued his come-play-with-me call. Intrigued by the happy invite, the cat cautiously made her way back to the deck. Mooshie pulled a pawful of kibbles out of the bowl and batted a few in her direction. She ate a couple, then batted the rest back at him, which triggered a feline food fight.

I named the stray Seizon-sha, Japanese for survivor. She kept her distance from me but loved hanging out with Mooshie. Initially she showed considerable curiosity over Mooshie's halter and leash, but before long, treated it with the same nonchalance one might assume with a family member who wore a prosthetic limb.

*

Salem was my guide in all things Montserratian, and a better teacher I could not have found for love or money. His pearls of Montserratian wisdom were wonderfully practical, like the time he found me doing the laundry and told me that if an islander did a load of laundry more than once every three months, that person was wearing too many clothes.

One beautiful afternoon in May, Salem paid me a welcomed visit. His lesson plan for the day was jumbies—his favorite subject. He escorted me from one end of the property to the other, pointing out the exact trees where the jumbies lived. Lowering his voice in a conspiratorial whisper, he leaned close to my ear. "Ahlll right now woman, I tell you true. Dey jumbies hear us searching for dem and dey go hide. It's dem snakes and cats, every one o' dem a jumbie. I tellin' you, woman, evil 'tings dey be. I don't ask no'ting 'bout no jumbie. Don't want to know jumbie name, 'cause if dey tells me dey name, dat make me brother to dat jumbie. I say don't have no'ting to do wit dey cats and dey snakes. I cut dem fast—dey don't talk to nobody."

In the silence that immediately followed this lecture, Mooshie called for me from his prison in our bedroom closet where I'd unceremoniously thrown him after I heard Salem's machete clanking on the low stone fence that bordered the path up to the house—the Montserratian's polite way of letting me know he was approaching.

I don't know if it was something Mooshie remembered from the strawberry flat smuggling episode, or if it was my panicked reaction every time I heard someone coming toward the house, my cat knew that whenever other people came around, it was important he stay quiet and out of sight. Except on this day he obviously forgot.

I held my breath.

Salem took a few steps in the direction of the downstairs deck, his eyes wide. "You hear dat?"

Snapping out of my panic, I laughed then mimicked Mooshie's cry to a tee, praying that Mooshie wouldn't want to chat in cat language as we sometimes did. I never fully understood what the subjects of our conversations were, but as a rule, Mooshie usually went away satisfied, as though something had been settled in his favor.

Salem gaped. "Do dat again."

I imitated Mooshie's call a few more times, walking as

fast as was politely possible, away from the house and toward the main road.

"That old bush medicine woman who lives out by the Soufrière taught me how to tell the jumbies to stay clear of me and this house in the cat language," I explained.

This was the truth, except the piercing cry she taught me was closer to the scream of a peacock than a cat's meow.

Salem shook his head, obviously pained by my explanation. "Don't you be sayin' no'ting to dem jumbies or dey come in da night and suck da breath outta you body."

Feigning fear, I bit the inside of my cheek to keep from laughing at the thought of the hundreds of times Mooshie nearly smothered me in my sleep by lying across my face.

Mooshie called again, this time louder.

Before I could stop him, Salem was striding for the deck with me on his heels. I talked fast, spinning a crazy yarn about working as a ventriloquist in my spare time.

Intent on hunting down a live jumbie, Salem wasn't listening. He took the deck steps three at a time and jerked to a halt at the top. I bumped into him and bounced back a step. The blood drained from Salem's face as he glowered at something on the deck, his expression one of loathing.

Afraid that Mooshie might have used his Houdini talents to escape the closet, I peered around Salem, already planning on how I would throw myself over Mooshie and beg for mercy for my jumbie.

What I saw instead of my sunbathing cat was a sizable Antilles racer snake.

I instantly reached for it. I could say that I did this because I didn't want to see such a beautiful and beneficial reptile killed—which is true, but it is also true that whenever I see a snake, my first impulse is to pick it up.

I should have learned my lesson about picking up snakes from an incident that took place years before. I was running on a remote mountain trail in California and came upon a snake lying across my path. It didn't move so I checked the tip of its tail for a rattle, saw none, and, thinking the reptile dead, picked it up for closer inspection. I was holding the snake four inches from my face when I heard a faint *sssssssss*.

The rattle-less tail was vibrating. The snake's lower jaw dropped open so wide I saw past the delicately curved white fangs and flicking tongue, all the way down its pink throat. It was only when it drew back its head and hissed like a cat that my brain registered the reality of the situation: *Baby rattlesnake! Fling it away!*

My fingers were less than an inch from the racer when I saw the flash of Salem's machete as it rose. I flicked my fingers and the racer took off, escaping the blade by an eighth of an inch.

Salem was shaking, plainly frightened. For one chilling moment I thought he was going to accuse me of having the power to call jumbies. Instead, he sat down hard on the deck lounge and ran a hand over his face.

"You see dat snake?"

I nodded, trying to determine what had so upset the Montserratian. "But Salem, surely you've run into common racer snakes before."

183

Salem violently shook his head. "Dat no common snake. Dat a snake jumbie wit a cat jumbie *inside* him. Dat be double bad." He stood abruptly. "I go tell me brother now. We go find dat double jumbie right away quick.

"You don't call to dem jumbies no more, okay?"

I answered with a smile and a double thumbs up.

Salem turned and disappeared into the rainforest in pursuit of the soon-to-be-famous Double Jumbie.

The moment he was out of sight, my anxiety level dropped enough that I was able to detach my shoulders from my ears. Rescuing my cat from the closet, I kissed his head and massaged between his toes until he purred.

I held him at eye level. "And no more calling out to your fellow jumbies either, you got that pal?"

Mooshie pressed his nose to my lips and chirped his agreement.

*

The next time Salem came to visit, it was not to give a lesson, but rather a warning. He'd gone at length about how I needed to pay close attention to the creatures of the jungle. The way he put it was, "If dey birds don't sing, and dey creatures hide, dat mean bad wind come. Wind be evil jumbies breathin' hard, wantin' to smite you down!"

I was struck by how closely this mirrored something my father often said on our many treks through the forests of upstate New York: "The best naturalist is the one who notices the hidden and the insignificant."

Same advice, different words.

It wasn't long after Salem's visit that I awoke to a hot day that was still as death. The usual cacophony of birdsong and insects had been replaced with the sound of wind blowing through the trees. Sure that we were in for another heavy rainstorm, I wasn't too concerned. If I could deal with tropical storms as a tourist, I was sure I could weather them as a resident. Besides, a nice refreshing downpour would be welcomed.

I didn't give Salem's warning a second thought, though I do remember staring out at the overcast sky and thinking, *Gosh, what a pretty shade of green.*

It was my cat, not me, who intuited what was happening—again proving he was the smarter half of our interspecies couple. Sometime during the early morning hours, Mooshie had tunneled under the mosquito netting of our bed, ripped open the thin covering of the box springs, and crawled inside. He refused to come to me, moving further out of range of my hand.

Other than telling me about evil jumbies breathing hard, Salem had yet to teach me about the ways of hurricanes and severe tropical storms. I had no idea that summer and fall were hurricane and tropical storm seasons. Neither did I know that these forces of nature could come on quickly and with only a few subtle warnings . . . like a greenish cast to the sky and an unnatural stillness.

Let me reiterate: I *am* perfectly capable of being a moron.

I left Mooshie to skulk inside the box springs and went to make our morning tea. Heading up the stairs, I glanced at the barometer needle and cocked my head. The needle seemed lower than usual. Mr. Partch, my unflappable seventh-grade science teacher, taught us about falling barometric pressures, but for the life of me, I couldn't remember any of it.

By the time I finished my tea, the wind had increased exponentially and the needle on the barometer had dropped even lower. There was a menacing undertone to the air, and the decrease in air pressure was beginning to do unkind things to my eardrums.

I again attempted to remove Mooshie from the box springs and this time he took a swipe at my hand and hissed. His uncharacteristic behavior prompted me to take a closer look at him. I was shocked to see that he was trembling and his pupils were fully dilated.

I came out from under the bed in time to see the sky open and let loose sheets of rain so heavy I couldn't see anything beyond the deck.

Mooshie yowled.

I ripped my computer away from its cables and shoved it into a plastic clothes bag. I then upended the mattress, dug my cat out of the box springs, and hustled upstairs to collect his carrier from the main hall closet. At the top of the stairs, I was transfixed by the tropical reenactment of *The Wizard of Oz* tornado scene going on in the main room. Furniture was moving on its own, and the dishes and pans were rattling out of their cabinets.

Mooshie forced his head into my armpit. Prying him off me, I pushed him into the carrier then wrapped an old blanket around it. While I crawled from one bank of hurricane shutters to the next, securing them as I went, a section of the roof blew off and smashed into the breadfruit tree. It was time to go.

In the garage, I found the motorcycle helmet Salem gave me in trade for a tire pump and strapped it on. Securing the carrier and my computer to my body with a canvas luggage strap, I crawled on all fours across the side yard to the ten by twelve solid concrete shed known as "the strong room."

Barricaded between the old wringer-style washer and a concrete utility sink, Mooshie and I clung to each other for the next four hours while the wind raged around us. I rubbed Mooshie's paws and read to him from a moldy, snail-slimed copy of *Popular Mechanics* that I found under a bucket used to keep the door open.

When we emerged from the strong room, I was surprised to find the house still standing. The landscape, however, appeared to have been rearranged by a gigantic blender. I grew tired just thinking of the amount of time and work it would take to get the grounds back into shape.

As for the deck chairs, tables, sun umbrellas, and pool floats, I never saw hide nor hair of them again.

*

Those first days following the storm were tough for my jumbie. Seizon-sha disappeared, leaving Mooshie's playdate calls unanswered.

Our electric service was out and I harbored no false hopes that it would be restored any time soon. The stove and oven were fueled by propane, so I at least had the luxury of hot food and water. On the other hand, if the stove had been electric, I wouldn't have had the opportunity to poison myself.

Food was one of the challenges I faced on the island. As a carnivore, Mooshie always had access to a good supply of fresh meat and fish, but I was a longtime vegetarian, and locating fresh produce was not always easy. I tried several times to grow my own vegetables, but the agouties found the seedlings particularly delicious. Plymouth's open-air market did provide me with onions, squash, and peppers, but leafy greens and other cruciferous veggies were harder to come by.

I was foraging among the vegetation on the estate, hoping to find a substitute for lettuce, when I discovered several cashew trees tucked back in a corner of the property. Thinking I could easily roast my own, I harvested the ripe cashew apples and removed the nuts from the bottoms.

Visions of sitting on the veranda with a bowl of hot roasted cashews clouded my good sense. Instead of asking the locals about how, or even *if* one could process the cashews that grew in our yards, I put two full pans of raw cashew nuts into the oven and set it for roasting.

I remained excited by the prospect of eating something that I'd harvested, right up until blue smoke and noxious fumes came billowing out of the oven vents. I managed to splash the black oil in which the nuts were now swimming all over myself as I siphoned it off. With my proclivity for experimenting with natural oils on my skin, it's a wonder I didn't try rubbing the stuff into my face and neck.

The entire mess ended up buried deep under a patch of barren land. It wasn't until years later that I learned that the processing of cashews is a labor-intensive and dangerous endeavor due to the toxic acids in the shell. Who knew?

Obviously not me, because a few hours after the failed roasting attempt, I awoke in distress, a prisoner inside my red, itching, and swollen body. For the two weeks that I lay covered head to toe in baking soda paste (for the itching), I kept my body's allergic responses in check with prednisone and Benadryl. To keep myself sane, I read every book in the house, including the phone directory.

When my supply of books finally petered out, the idea of returning to the States sneaked through the backdoor of my mind, took a seat, and refused to leave. I tried to ignore it, but it teased me like a relentless mosquito until I was forced to take an honest look at our life on Montserrat.

The Emerald Isle of the Caribbean was indeed a paradise, unspoiled by overdevelopment, violence, greed, and pollution. And while it was true that living in the middle of such tropical splendor far from the madding crowd had been a lifelong dream come true, there were drawbacks to be reckoned with.

The most crucial of these thorns among the mangos was the threat of Mooshie being discovered and "stashed" with one swing of a machete.

Next was my computer which would undoubtedly shut down sooner than later and leave me without access to my work files. As far as I knew, there were few, if any, computers on the island, let alone computer repair techs to fix them.

The absence of cleared trails made running impossible, and I refused to run on the winding narrow roadways where the speed limit was a matter of personal choice. I purchased a jog belt so I could run in the pool but I soon realized that running in water was a far cry from running on terra firma.

And okay, I'll admit it—there were times I missed having easy access to the things I took for granted in the States—libraries, bookstores, a well-stocked supermarket, computer techs, a modern hospital.

The moment I'd begin fretting over these things, I'd search out my cat who, being a cat and totally unconcerned with such matters, could usually be found lazing happily in the sun. I'd then take in a breath of fresh, clean air, look out over the sea, and scold myself for being such a weenie.

I was a writer for gods sake; I wanted the experience of being without all the conveniences and surfeit of "stuff" that Americans surrounded themselves with. In my family of origin, I was the "fixer" child—I welcomed the challenge of making the best of whatever trying situations came my way. I had a whole toolbox of wilderness *and* urban survival skills I'd learned at my father's knee. My Montserratian women friends were more than willing to show me where to find and prepare the edible and medicinal plants and herbs that grew wild on the island.

When it came to the shortage of books, which were as necessary to my life as breathing, I devised a plan wherein a group of book lovers and I would set up a book swap and donation station in Plymouth for islanders and tourists alike. To bulk up the supply, we could call on our friends in the States and the U.K. to periodically send boxes of books they'd already read.

As far as my furry jumbie and the machete menace was concerned, I reasoned that the house was set in a remote section of the island, and Salem never failed to announce himself, allowing me adequate time to conceal Mooshie. Any other visitors I might have had wouldn't think of stopping by without calling first.

And, in a pinch, I did have a few trusted friends who would gladly take Mooshie in and safeguard him in the unlikely event I needed to go off island. In the meantime, I would begin Salem's education on the positive attributes of certified jumbie-free cats.

Ultimately, if all else failed, I always had the option of flying to nearby Antigua where the services and supplies my cat or I might need could certainly be found.

During those weeks of recovery while I concentrated on the particulars of our lives on the island, life in the rest of the world was marching on. Events of which I had only a passing knowledge were taking place in Los Angeles. If I'd had the ability to see into the future, I would have seen that I needn't have worried about which path Mooshie's and my life should take—the jurors who served on the Rodney King trial helped make that decision for us.

*

Whenever I frequented the small shops in Plymouth during the time of that infamous trial, I would invariably find Montserratians crowded around a newspaper or radio, talking about the latest developments in the case. It was plain to see from their uncharacteristically grave expressions that the Rodney King trial meant something far more consequential to them than an entertaining American courtroom drama.

At the time, I thought the Montserratians' preoccupation with the case was directly related to the discriminatory and degrading manner in which they were treated by the more bigoted and narrow-minded of the tourists and expats.

In the wake of the trial, The negative effect the verdict had on the native peoples of the West Indies was far-reaching. Among the Montserratians, long buried resentments rose to the surface. I don't know if it was in solidarity with American Blacks or not, but racial tension on the island increased and culminated in a printed demand that the whites leave the island.

From where I stood, I didn't blame the Montserratians for feeling as they did. I was proud that they had found their voice and exercised their right to use it.

Living outside the center of island gossip and activity, Mooshie and I escaped the worst of the initial rancor, although as the political turmoil gathered force, the effects would eventually reach us as well. Basic services were suspended, and goods were scarce. We managed, but still I kept a low profile hoping things would settle down and reconstructive communications could begin. When they didn't, and my friends, both Montserratian and white, began to leave, I reluctantly made the decision to follow.

*

Moving Mooshie off the island proved much easier than smuggling him in. I simply purchased tickets on a commercial Caribbean airliner for my under-twelve traveling companion, Mr. Mushu P. Heron. I doubted anyone would care that my companion preferred to travel in a small plastic box.

For our remaining weeks on Montserrat, I thoroughly cleaned the house and, with Salem's help, spruced up the grounds. On our last day in residence, I prepared a feast of Mooshie's favorite foods served with plenty of English Breakfast tea. I carried a tray laden with goodies to his room only to find the bathroom shutters pushed open and my feline Houdini gone.

Besieged by images of my cat under attack by an army of machetes, or drowned in one of the island's many ghauts, I searched the tropical rainforest that surrounded the house. Perhaps like Dowie, the veteran *Lusitania* cat that abandoned ship the night before her fatal voyage, Mooshie's feline instincts told him our upcoming journey was ill-fated as well.

Exhausted and miserable, I pressed my face into a pillow and screamed like a lunatic in a rubber room until a familiar squeak came through the usual cacophony of night critters.

I got out the last can of kitty smack snacks and shook it. There came another squeak. The shake-squeak, shake-squeak echolocation process went on until I was led to the liquor cabinet. I aimed the beam of my flashlight over the dark corners of the interior. Two luminous green orbs jumped out at me. I cried with relief, berating myself for not noticing him when I closed the cabinet doors after wiping them down with lemon oil earlier in the day.

That night my cat feasted on fresh minced chicken breast, tuna and tea. By the time he nestled into his spot between my chin and shoulder, he was a purring butterball. He intuited that we were about to be on the move again and I am certain he was glad to be going.

The Montserratians at the airport regarded Mooshie's carrier with an air of suspicion. One older gentleman, egged on by his dice-throwing companions, warily approached us.

"What ting you got in dey box, sistah?"

I hesitated, pondering the list of possible answers. "Well brother," I said in the most serious tone I could muster, "I tell you true—it is a cat that I have captured for scientific study on the mainland."

With perfect timing, Mooshie pushed his foreleg through a hole, his claws fully extended. I admit it *did* look unearthly.

The man stepped back and crossed himself, mumbling something in the Montserratian patois. The only word I heard clearly was "jumbie."

The group casually resumed their dice game and never gave me or the carrier another glance. I guessed that as long as the jumbie was going *off* the island with his white obeah witch, they weren't about to get their machetes in a twist.

· 12 ·

OF BUFOS AND BULLETS

"As anyone who has ever been around a cat for any length of time well knows, cats have enormous patience with the limitations of the human kind."
— Cleveland Amory, *The Cat Who Came for Christmas*

Mooshie and I had the Puerto Rico apartment to ourselves while Julie was in Seattle visiting her fiancé. My grand plan was to stay there for two weeks while I lined up living arrangements in California. I should have known better, or at least heard the gods laughing at my silly attempts to plan ahead. Like something out of a fairy tale, the unintentional architect of the new plan which would steer our lives in a whole different direction was a six-inch toad.

The week before our arrival in Puerto Rico the island had been plagued by tropical storms that knocked out the electricity over most of the island. Many people, ourselves included, were still without power.

Heat and humidity do not make for easy sleeping, which

is why I was sprawled out on the cool living room floor tiles at two a.m. reading by candlelight.

Mooshie trudged in from the rain-washed patio and sat next to my head. Absently, I reached over and stroked him.

"What's going on, little man?" I turned to look at him and my breath caught in my throat.

His eyes were covered by the inner opaque lid that Dr. Petrie called the nictitating membrane—the sign of a seriously ill cat. Mooshie opened his mouth in a silent cry and fell onto his side, his legs twitching uncontrollably.

My mind racing, I wrapped him in a towel and called a taxi service. I stumbled through our address and explained where I needed to go. The dispatcher heard the urgency in my voice and promised in broken English to send someone right away.

At two fifteen a.m., Mooshie's breathing grew labored. Holding him close, I paced the street outside our building, alternately cursing the taxi driver and begging Mooshie not to die. It didn't take a medical professional to know that the longer he went without medical intervention, the less the chance he had of surviving.

Ten minutes later we were in a beat-up Ford Granada racing toward the only all-night emergency pet hospital in Puerto Rico. The driver of the makeshift taxi, a scary looking guy with a scar that ran down the left side of his face, solemnly described our destination as being in a "bad neighborhood." From what I'd seen of the neighborhoods we'd already passed, I couldn't imagine how it could get any worse.

Mooshie lay against my chest. Every few minutes he would have a mini seizure, then go quiet. I'd seen a lot of humans die in the same manner.

I begged the driver to go faster, tearfully explaining over the din of the engine that my *gato* was dying. He wasn't just any *gato* off the street—he was *un gato extraordinario.*

I was still urging the cabbie on when I heard four quick popping sounds and the ping of something hitting the back bumper. *Firecrackers,* I thought. *Must be a festival for one of the patron saints.*

I briefly wondered which patron saint was being celebrated when the taxi accelerated and the driver yelled at me to get down on the floor. Confused, I didn't immediately react—at least not until a bullet shattered the rear window. I slid to the floor with Mooshie just in time to see the driver pull a sawed-off shotgun from under his seat and blindly aim it out his window. Only then did it dawn on me that we were in the middle of gang warfare.

"Don't you *dare* go anywhere else except the pet hospital!" I screamed, afraid the cabbie would veer off course to outrun our pursuers. In answer, a spray of shattered glass landed on my back. Pulling my raincoat over my head, I curled around my cat until the car came to a jarring halt.

"Vamos!" the driver shouted. "Get out! Go!"

I flung open the door and jumped into the street. The taxi peeled out, fishtailing in a cloud of smoke, the rear door still open. I ran to the only lighted building on the block.

The hand-printed cardboard sign taped to the door read:

Clínica de Emergencies Animal. I opened the door to a waiting room full of extremely sober-looking people, but no animals. For a second or two I thought the driver had misunderstood and dropped me off at a walk-in clinic for depressed humans—either that or a three a.m. Alcoholics Anonymous meeting. Then I heard the weak whining bark of a dog in his death throes.

At the back of the room, a woman wearing scrubs patterned with pink cats and blue dogs motioned to me. In a torrent of words and sobs, I explained what had happened. When I mentioned the part about Mooshie's seizures and his inability to walk, she swiftly produced a towel-lined basket, indicating that I should put him into it.

I laid my cat's limp body on the towel. He was no longer moving, and for one horrifying second, I thought he was dead. Everything around me disappeared. I saw nothing except the image of my cat lying on a red towel.

The woman whisked the basket away and disappeared behind a shabby curtain. The sudden absence of Mooshie felt like an essential part of me had been torn away. Behind that curtain, he'd be surrounded by strange people, suffering dogs, and terrible smells. He'd be alone without me. Or, more accurately, I'd be alone without him. There was no way I would let my cat die afraid and alone in some cold and antiseptic room.

Pushing the curtain aside, I stepped into a hallway.

The woman swiveled around and pointed to a sign written in both Spanish and English: NO ADMITTANCE! AUTHORIZED PERSONNEL ONLY!

"You no come in here!" she snapped in the same voice of authority that I so often used in the emergency room. "Go sit in the waiting room!"

I started to explain that my cat could not be separated from his human, but the words were strangled as I began to sob.

Her voice softened. "The doctor, he will come to see you after he examines your cat. You wait. Pray to the Holy Virgin. Let the doctor do his job." With that, she turned and disappeared with the love of my life.

I sat in the waiting room for what felt like an eternity, listening to the whimpering dog and the low murmurs of those who were trying to save their patients. When the voices and the dog fell silent, I knew it wasn't good news for the dog.

It turned out that all seven people in the waiting room belonged to the dog that died. The veterinarian, a man who didn't look a day over fifteen, gave them the news first in fluent Spanish, and then in English.

All in all, I thought they took it well. No one screamed or fell to their knees wailing—just as I would do if it were Mooshie.

For the next three hours, I flipped between torturous thoughts of losing Mooshie and positive thoughts that he would pull through. When I couldn't stand it any longer, I headed for the forbidden world behind the curtain. My hand was on the curtain when the vet swept into the waiting room. He explained that Mooshie was alive—but barely.

"The dog that died tonight ate the same type of

poisonous toad that your cat probably tangled with on your patio."

"A toad? Are you saying a toad caused this?"

He nodded. "Bufo marinus toads are drawn out into the open during the rains. A good number of dogs and cats die every year from eating or licking them.

"Your cat is lucky. I doubt he directly ingested the toxin for the simple reason that if he had, he'd be dead." He hesitated then shrugged. "But I can't guarantee that he won't die. I've stabilized him for now with IV fluids and medications, but you need to take him to his regular vet as soon as they open this morning. This is only an emergency clinic. Your cat needs more than what we can do for him here."

"I don't have a regular vet," I said. "We don't live here."

He asked where I was staying then jotted down the name and address of a veterinarian near our apartment building. "This office opens in about an hour. We'll call a taxi for you and have them take you directly there."

He pulled a sheet of paper off his clipboard and handed it to me. "This is what we've done to treat him so far; make sure you give this to the vet. Your cat won't drink or eat for a while, so he'll need an IV. The sooner he gets one, the better off he'll be."

The receptionist appeared holding Mooshie. The opaque eyelids were still visible, but he lifted his head long enough to recognize me and open his mouth in a weak cry.

Outside I whispered soothing words into Mooshie's fur

until the same bullet-riddled taxi that dropped us off arrived to pick us up.

*

Dr. Rodriguez, a kind and compassionate soul, confirmed that Mooshie was still in touch-and-go condition and that a continuous IV infusion of fluids was necessary to keep him alive. He suggested that the best place for my cat would be in the States in a modern, fully equipped veterinary hospital.

California would be too long and strenuous a trip, but my father lived in upstate New York. We could hop on a plane and be at Albany Airport in a few hours. I smiled for the first time since the nightmare began.

"He needs to be carefully watched," Dr. Rodriguez warned. "I have no one here at night to do that. You can you do this, sí?"

I nodded. "I am a nurse—*Soy enfermera.* Tell me what I need to do."

Dr. Rodriguez smiled and nodded as he went about gathering supplies. "I will start the IV. Watch how I do it so that when your cat pulls it out, you can start a new IV on the other leg. I will give you what you need to do this."

I wasn't expecting that. Starting an intravenous line on humans in crisis was one thing, starting one on a puny, dehydrated cat that I adored, scared the hell out of me.

Seeing my apprehension, Dr. Rodriguez moved the overhead surgical lamp directly over Mooshie's foreleg. He then showed me where to find the best veins and how to hold my cat's leg while inserting the needle. He then shaved an identical area on Mooshie's other foreleg in preparation for the IV I would have to start.

I called the man St. Francis and thanked him profusely. When the receptionist handed me the bill, I was stunned. The amount was a fraction of what Dr. Petrie would have charged. It seemed like such a small price to pay in exchange for my cat's life. I wrote out a check for triple the amount and considered it the most worthwhile donation I'd ever made.

For two days and nights, I alternated between dozing and watching the drips in Mooshie's IV chamber. He slept most of the time, raising his head only long enough to croak out a faint meow. On the second night, he dislodged his IV while using his litterbox.

In all my years as a nurse, I had never felt as accomplished as I did when I successfully started an IV on my cat by candlelight.

Four days later, Mooshie lapped up an ounce of bottled water and ate one mouthful of ground chicken. Not wanting to take any chances, I let his IV run right up until we entered the jetway for our flight north.

Mooshie spent the entire flight curled up on my lap, snoring the exhausted snore of a cat that had won a major backyard brawl. I stroked his head, my eyes fixed on his chest rising and falling. I couldn't even guess what life held in store for us, but I looked forward to having a long time together to figure it out.

PART FOUR

ANIMAL SHELTER

· 13 ·

YOU *CAN* GO HOME AGAIN— AND THEN LEAVE

"The smallest feline is a masterpiece."
— Leonardo da Vinci (1452 – 1519)

'Tis a strange thing to be a middle-aged adult and living with your elderly parent in the same house where you once watched *The Howdy Doody Show* and *I Love Lucy*. This was both a blessing and a disappointment—a blessing because Mooshie and I were with my dad and we had a roof over our heads; and a disappointment in that it somehow meant I had failed not only myself but my cat as well.

My father was a gentle, fun-loving Italian in his eighties who still worked full time—not because he had to, but because he didn't know how else to be. For Mooshie and my dad, it was love at first sight. From the moment Mooshie crawled into my father's arms, the two were inseparable. They ate together, took walks, and watched

Jeopardy and reruns of the *Lawrence Welk Show*. My father spoke to him in Italian, and Mooshie, a bilingual cat, answered in Italian—*Brrrriti!*

After many long delays and complications, *Mercy* had at last been published. Not wanting to let too much grass grow under my feet, I did what I'd always done in the face of uncertainty—I wrote. Staking out writing territory in the attic, I purchased a desk, lamp, and chair at a garage sale. I then plunged into writing my third book, *Condition Critical,* the sequel to *Intensive Care.*

I was euphoric about being able to run again. My mind churned out a surprising number of ideas and character profiles as I ran. I often found myself running to the rhythm of sentences I created as I went—sometimes taking steps backward as if to erase the last few words and start again. For what remained of the summer and early fall, I wrote in our baking hot attic while Mooshie practiced heat-induced narcolepsy next to my keyboard.

Every year for as long as I could remember, my father would rent a plot of land along the banks of the Mohawk River and fill it with rows of vegetables, herbs, and flowers. When I wasn't writing, I helped with the weeding, watering, and harvesting while Mooshie chased butterflies and bees.

It was during corn harvest that my cat discovered a new unconventional food obsession—corncobs. No matter how deep we buried them in the compost pile, my cat would root around until he found one. Hunkering down, he'd sink his teeth into it, and drag it into a corner. There, he would rip into the cob with all the ferociousness of a lion bringing down an antelope. And god help the person who tried to take the cob away from him. If anyone came too near his prize, he'd show his claws and give the interloper a look that could freeze both man and beast in their tracks.

Every so often his snaggletooth would get stuck in the core of the cob. Far from being bothered by it, he would walk around the house with it hanging off his tooth, proudly showing off his latest cob conquest.

With time, Mooshie's corncob obsession faded into indifference. Knowing that boredom was soon to follow, I decided the yard would be the perfect diversion for him. My family home was located on a sizable corner lot that my father had populated with a variety of trees and a plethora of exotic plants and flowers. Each morning Mooshie was clipped into his harness and allowed to roam among them.

The long whip-like branches of the weeping willows taunted my feline like a feathered-wand cat toy. Hooded under the umbrella of hanging branches, he'd leap straight up, pull down a branch, strip it of leaves, then move on to the next one.

Leaving my feline ward to the willows, I returned to my attic atelier secure in the knowledge that my father would be keeping an eye on him. It wasn't an hour later that the sound of my father's laughter drew me like a magnet to the kitchen.

In the middle of the floor, my cat lay on his back, all four paws in the air. His pupils were dilated and there were blobs of drool forming at the corners of his mouth. Shreds of what appeared to be fresh marijuana covered his fur and flecked his tongue, which was dangling out the side of his mouth.

Seeing me, he spun around in a circle, flung himself down with force, wrestled with his tail, then viciously thumped it with his back paws. He then swiveled around the floor, jumped onto the counter, bit the calendar hanging from the cabinet door, and threw himself down onto the floor again.

I was leaning over to examine the green vegetable matter when Mooshie hurled himself at my hand, pinning it with his claws. The freakish sounds that came out of him were new, as if a being from outer space had found a home in his voice box.

I marveled as he flipped onto his back again and slithered like a rat snake first one way, then another.

"Jeez Dad, what the hell did you do to him?"

"He found the catnip," my father explained, wiping away tears of laughter. "I plant it for the neighborhood cats. It makes them happy."

I looked at my father in disbelief. "He's mentally unstable as it is, Dad. I don't think he needs any recreational drugs to help him find his way to insanity." I considered telling my father about my cat's excursion into alcoholism and his smack snack addiction, but didn't want to put a damper on his illusions of Mooshie as the perfect cat.

On the other side of the kitchen, my cat stuck his paw into the crack between the fridge and the counter and pulled out a stray rigatoni. He proceeded to bat the pasta around the floor at hyperspeed. When he started bouncing off the cabinet doors, my father beamed with delight.

"You see? It doesn't hurt him and he has a good time."

I took my father by the shoulders. "Dad, I hate to tell you this, but you sound like a drug dealer. Look at him—he's out of his mind."

We both turned our attention on Mooshie, who was now standing on his hind legs juggling the rigatoni while his tongue hung out the side of his mouth.

"I can't believe this, Dad. You've always been against drugs."

"Sure, for humans. For Mooshie—a little taste of crazy does him good."

Doubtfully, I observed my cat who was now rolling in the catnip shreds.

"But Dad, you—"

My father patted my arm. "Don't worry, it's alright. Enjoy your cat having fun. In a few minutes the catnip will overtake him and he will fall over and sleep for a long time."

My father started for the back door.

"Where are you going?"

"I'm going to pick a pound of catnip leaves and dry them. That way Mooshie will always have a ready supply of crazy for years to come."

*

We finished harvesting the garden, dried the basil, oregano, and tomato seeds, and put away the gardening tools. Mooshie and I moved out of the attic and into one of the three empty upstairs bedrooms.

When the chilling rains descended on us without mercy, Mooshie lost all interest in going outside. He grew increasingly restless and soon took to wandering around the house with one of his stuffed mice hanging from his left lower canine. When boredom set in, he amused himself by knocking things off my desk or the kitchen counters just to see them fall and smash into little pieces that he would then bat around the floor.

I didn't blame him. Feeling antsy, I took to running four-mile circuits a few times a day. This allowed plenty of thinking time to work out the kinks in the new book and figure out what the next phase of our lives should look like.

It was during one of these runs that I came across a 1978 Grand LeMans Safari woody station wagon with a for sale sign in the window. The first time I slipped in behind the wheel I fell in love with the cushioned bench seats and power steering. My initial test drive around the village was like driving a comfy living room couch while watching *Route 66*. Eight hundred dollars later, the sofa on wheels was mine.

I'd never been to Florida, but for years my friends and acquaintances who either visited or lived in the Sunshine State assured me that I'd hate it. Enticed by these prophecies and the fact that Florida was fifty degrees warmer than New York, it was clear that it was time for another adventure. Before the first flakes of snow could hit the ground, I bid my father *arrivederci,* packed up my computer, prepared a thermos of tea, slid Mooshie into his carrier, and aimed the Pontiac's hood ornament to the south.

Despite promises of sun and stifling heat, Mooshie complained for the entire 1300-mile trip. Never once while the car was rolling, did he stop. By the time I caught sight of the fifty-by-thirty-foot Confederate flag that waved over the interstate in southwest Florida, I was seriously contemplating drugs—first for me, then my cat.

When I began matching Mooshie yowl for yowl, I got off the highway and followed the road to a drawbridge that landed us on a barrier island in the Gulf of Mexico. The following day I rented a furnished downstairs flat in a house that was known to the locals as Fishermen Flats.

Mooshie made a home for himself on the back of a ratty chair set in front of the windows facing the boat harbor. This roost provided him with patches of sun in which to soak for most of the day. Being on display, he soon attracted the attention of the resident group of commercial fishermen who passed by our window on their way to and from their boats.

I'm not sure if it was the smell of fish or his need for male bonding, but within a month Mooshie was performing for the group, standing on his hind legs, nose pressed against the window glass.

At first the men snickered and kept on walking, but after a few days, they started tapping on the window. On cue, the feline attention junkie rolled onto his back and squirmed around like a freshly caught fish. He pawed the air, his pink tongue lolling out the side of his mouth. To assure himself that his audience was still watching, he would pause long enough to give the group a series of happy chirps and meows.

Thinking a dose of one-on-one male bonding would be good for him, I let Mooshie out on his leash before the fishermen returned each day. The fishermen were a tougher group than I'd bargained for. The first few days they walked right by him making mocking meow noises that any self-respecting cat would resent.

Within a few days of not receiving the fawning attention he felt was his due, Mooshie took a running leap, clawed his way up one man's leg to his shoulders, and clamped onto his ear. This brought about a riot of hooting, hollering, and general bobbery.

The next day, one of the fishermen presented my cat with a baitfish. Mooshie sniffed the thing, batted it around, and then carried it to the side yard, leaving it where the fishermen would be sure to see it—my cat's version of regifting.

The next time the fishermen came through, they brought him a perfectly filleted fish. Mooshie tore off a piece, ate it, and ignored the rest. Cat-to-English translation: nice try, but no cigar.

The following day, the fishermen served His Lordship a hungry man portion of grilled grouper, deboned and cut into perfect small bites.

Greedily hunkering over his dream meal, Mooshie's eyes dilated and his front paw, claws extended, flew out at the speed of light to cover his treasure.

Intrigued by Mooshie's response, one fisherman stepped closer.

Mooshie's primal snarl distinctly translated as, *Back off if you value your face, Fishboy!* It had the desired effect. With perfect Rockettes-style timing, the fishermen stepped back as a unit.

His Lordship wolfed down the grouper in seconds, then stood and regarded his incredulous fans, his mouth covered in grilled grouper bits. Taking the opportunity to show off his multiple personalities, he put his meerkat persona into action by standing on his hind legs and paddling the air with his front paws.

The fishermen, not known for their warm and fuzzy demeanors, were grinning and all talking at once like little kids on their first visit to the zoo. Smart feline that he was, Mooshie had thus assured himself of a constant supply of fresh grilled grouper.

Not long after he cast his spell over the fishermen, I received a call from a friend in Marin asking if I could housesit her home for four months. To save on nerves— both mine and Mooshie's—I shipped the Pontiac, bade farewell to Fishermen Flats, and flew back to San Francisco to begin the next phase in our lives as professional free spirits.

· 14 ·

FREDDY KRUEGER AND THE
HOUSE SITTERS IS NOT A BAND

*"The problem with cats is that they get the same
exact look whether they see a moth or an ax-
murderer."*

— Paula Poundstone

Word spread quickly that Mooshie and I were available for long-term house, ranch, and farm sitting—free of charge. Not only did this way of life provide me with thought-provoking places to write, but the constant change of scenery kept Mooshie forever on his toes exploring new escape routes.

When the caretaking jobs became sporadic, I rented a one-bedroom duplex in Marin and settled in. The day after I sent the final version of *Condition Critical* to the publishers, I signed up for per diem work in several San Francisco critical care units.

It was around this time that Mooshie fell ill with what I called the Mystery Plague, a diabolical malady that crept up on my cat in three stages: progressive lethargy, loss of appetite, and finally, the rapid onset of high fever and the appearance of the opaque membranes covering his eyes.

That first time he came down with the Mystery Plague, I rushed him through the hell of Marin commuter traffic to Dr. Petrie's office. The vet was mystified. There was no poisonous toad to blame it on, and Mooshie's lab work showed nothing to indicate why he was as sick as he was. He was given IV hydration and amoxicillin, and after a few days, discharged. Within the week he was back to himself.

"A fluke," Dr. Petrie declared with a shrug of the shoulders. "It was probably some rogue bacteria he picked up."

And that was all it took to lull me back into my fantasy that Mooshie would live forever.

*

It didn't take long to realize that with my hefty rent, paying Simon's college expenses, and Mooshie's vet bills, there was no way I could make ends meet on my per diem salary.

It was Nice Ex-Boyfriend who, in the spring of 1994, found a job for me in Los Angeles working as a nurse on a Hollywood movie set. The pay was triple the amount I was making as a critical care nurse. Not only could I make some serious money in a short time, but I was practically dancing with delight over the prospect of all the bizarre and exciting material I was going to gather as fodder for my writing.

As the set nurse, I was required to be the first one on the set, and the last one to leave. Unwilling to leave my cat locked in a room alone for fourteen plus hours a day, I at once began my search for a sitter who could stay one step ahead of Mooshie and didn't mind pampering him. At one hundred dollars for each twenty-four-hour day, an extended-stay in-home cat sitter in the San Francisco Bay area was not an option.

Nice Ex-Boyfriend's new girlfriend was allergic to cats, and the rest of my friends all had legitimate excuses for why they couldn't take Mooshie in. I posted ads in the local papers and put up notices on every bulletin board I could find—all to no avail.

With one week left in which to find a cat minder, a friend of a friend's friend directed me to Mr. K, who managed a flat rate cat boarding service in his home, which was located a few hours north of Los Angeles.

Out of time and options, I called Mr. K, who told me yes, he could board my cat. I asked my top twenty questions, all of which he answered appropriately. He then listened patiently while I shared Mooshie's health details and described his various idiosyncrasies. Mr. K addressed each of my concerns so that by the end of the interview he'd given me all the assurances anyone could have wished for.

Seeing as his place was on the way to Los Angeles, it was agreed I would meet him at his house for the handoff of both cat and the seven-page Mooshie Care Handbook that was chock full of instructions and "must do" lists.

The day before our journey south, I shredded the tenderest parts of a freshly cooked game hen, garnished it with potato chips, and set the bowl before my cat. In the narrow margin of time between when he finished eating and when he slipped into his usual postprandial daze, I gave him the news.

"Listen, sweetheart," I cooed, "Mommy has to go away for a while to earn money so she can buy lots of raw tuna and cans of the cat smack snacks you love so much."

Sitting like a human in a nest of pillows, Mooshie regarded me with mild interest. He issued a low guttural meow that sounded like, *Yeah, so?*

"Well, you'll be staying in a new house where there will be others of your species, and a nice man who will tend to all your needs. There's even a cat run in his yard so you can go outside anytime you want. How does that sound?"

In answer, Mooshie yawned and commenced licking his nether parts. I could hear him saying, *Whatever. Just let me clean my balls in peace, okay?*

Satisfied that he understood there was a serious change coming down the pike, I sighed and snuggled up with my cat.

I found Mr. K's two-story bungalow without any trouble. Situated in a respectable middle-class neighborhood, the tidy front yard was full of healthy blooming rose bushes which were presently being trimmed by a plump older woman with fluffy white hair. Thinking she was Mrs. K, I introduced myself.

Smiling, she pulled off her gardening gloves. "I'm Lola,

Mr. K's neighbor. He asked me to tell you he's sorry for not being here to meet you, but he had a dental emergency and needed to go. I was here trimming his roses so he asked if I'd wait for you and watch over your cat until he gets back."

"Have you been neighbors for a long time?" I asked, hoping for a little more insight into the man.

The woman cocked her head. "I think I met him when he first moved here about two or three years ago. He seems like a nice man, though he does keep to himself quite a bit."

She leaned in and lowered her voice. "I think it's because of all the cats. They say that people who have a lot of cats are like that."

I considered engaging the woman in a conversation about who "they" were, and what exactly "like that" meant, but let it pass—I needed to get on the road if I wanted to reach L.A. before dark.

"Do you know if Mr. K was in the cat minding business before?"

Lola pinched her neck. It was obvious she wasn't prepared for an interrogation.

"I'm not sure, but when he hired me to prune his roses he did say he'd moved around a lot before coming here."

Still holding my gaze, she tried pulling the carrier from my hand, but I wasn't inclined to surrender it so easily.

"Don't worry, I'm sure your cat will be fine," she said with an easy smile. "I'll keep him company until Mr. K gets back."

I kissed Mooshie goodbye and got into my car. In the

rearview mirror, I saw Lola wave and walk around the side of the house with my cat. A slight twinge of unease wrapped itself around my throat and squeezed ever so lightly. Try as I might, I could not put my finger on what bothered me. Chalking it up to separation anxiety, I drove on to the City of Angels.

*

Living in Los Angeles is like living on another planet. If driving in L.A. at breakneck speeds at all hours of the day and night didn't put me over the edge, dealing with those who inhabited the place should have. Many of the industry folks I worked with were wonderful and interesting people, but there were a few that defied the laws of being human. If I had to describe them, *sensible, sane,* and *humble* would not be among the adjectives I'd use.

The work itself was mindless—cleaning and bandaging wounds, checking blood pressures and temperatures, dispensing over-the-counter medications, and making sure everyone was hydrated. Once it became known I was a "real nurse," I spent a fair amount of time answering medical and mental health-related questions, giving common sense medical advice, and repeatedly explaining to one of the costars why I could not comply with her daily requests for cocaine and hydromorphone.

Over the first three weeks Mooshie and I were separated, I'd left a series of messages for Mr. K and received only two short replies, both of which were thin assurances that everything was "just fine." I tried to take the man at his word, but my intuition told me that something wasn't right.

One month into the filming I got my first break when a particularly virulent flu knocked out three-quarters of the grips and gaffers. Spreading like a California wildfire, the virus hit the makeup and wardrobe folks next, and then took down the director and his assistant. As the only medical person on the set, I had both the authority and the obligation to shut the film down.

I took advantage of the five-day intermission to pay a surprise visit to Mr. K's to make sure everything really was "just fine." Getting on the road first thing the next morning, I arrived at Mr. K's house by noon.

I rang the doorbell. No answer. I knocked, and then banged on the door. When there was still no answer, I walked around to the backyard hoping to see the cat run and a fenced yard full of cat toys and climbing trees.

The yard was empty. No cat toys, no cat run. With a growing sense of alarm, I again banged on the front door using my fists.

Lola, her white hair billowing around her head like so much cottonwood fluff, came running across the street. I opened my mouth to ask if she'd seen Mr. K, but she put a finger to her lips and without a word pulled me around to the back.

Pale and out of breath, she turned to face me.

"Thank god you're here. I didn't know how to get in touch with you. I didn't know what to do."

"What's wrong?"

She shook her head, "I don't even know how to tell you. I'm—"

I gripped her arm. "My cat! Is he okay?"

"I . . . I don't know. Mr. K left the day before yesterday and said he'd be back in a few days. I asked who was going to care for the cats while he was gone, and he said they'd be okay on their own. That didn't seem right to me, but I didn't think it was my place to say anything.

"I'm sorry. I . . . it's just that well, the house is . . . it's . . ." She trailed off with an involuntary shudder.

"Take a deep breath. What's wrong with the house?"

"Last night I got worried about the cats being all alone, you know? I couldn't stop thinking about them so I thought I'd take just a peek to make sure they were okay.

"Mr. K keeps a spare key hidden in case of emergencies. He's mentioned it to me several times, saying that if there was ever an emergency while he was gone, I could go in. So last night I—" She grabbed my hand. "I shouldn't have done it, but I went into the house, and I—"

"Tell me!" My heart was pounding.

"It's awful in there. It's—"

"Give me the key," I demanded. "This *is* an emergency. I need to get my cat out of there."

Beset by nerves, the woman pinched her neck and looked away "I don't want to start any trouble. I don't know what he'll do if I—"

I summoned my nurse-in-charge voice. "Lola, if you do not unlock that door and let me in right this minute, I am going to call the police. You can go home, or wait out here, but whether you're here or not, I *will* get inside this house one way or another, and I *will* get my cat out of there today!"

She hesitated.

"Do you have grandchildren, Lola?" I didn't wait for a reply. "Imagine if one of your grandkids were in there and you didn't know if they were okay or not. What would *you* do?"

The woman's face changed. She nodded and handed me the key. "You're right. Go get your cat. I'll wait here by the door. I'm sorry, but I can't go in there again."

I was about to unlock the door when Lola put a hand on my arm. "It's awful in there. The smell is . . . well, you'll need to be strong."

"That's the least of my worries. I'm a nurse; there isn't much I haven't seen or smelled."

I entered the foyer and instantly pivoted on my heel. I crouched next to the rose bushes and retched. Lola was right—the stench of urine and feces combined with a rotting meat smell was overpowering.

She put a hand on my back. "Are you okay?"

I nodded and held up a finger. "Be right back." I made a mad dash to the car where I pulled a jar of Vicks VapoRub from my medical kit and spread the ointment over the inside of a surgical mask. Fitting it tight over my nose and mouth, I re-entered the house. Starting with the main floor, I raced through the rooms calling for Mooshie. I saw at least thirty or more cats, most of them skeletal and listless, their fur dull and matted.

Cat feces, vomit, and patches of crystalized cat urine covered every surface including the walls, floors, tables, stovetop, and kitchen counters. I was tempted to open the refrigerator, but good sense told me not to—I'd already seen enough to fuel my nightmares for months.

Upstairs, the door to my left opened onto a dark airless room where I found cages stacked floor to ceiling, their size suited more for guinea pigs than cats. I imagined an adult cat crammed inside of one with no room to stand or stretch, and came unglued.

Charging into the hall I began throwing open doors, calling for Mooshie. The last room at the end of the hall was devoid of furniture except for an overturned plastic chair in front of a narrow closet. On the grimy carpet lying in their own filth were eight or nine cats, all of them listless and emaciated. They barely lifted their heads when I entered the room.

I took in the scene, unable to process the senseless abuse of innocent animals. The brutality of it hit me like a physical blow. I knelt next to them and in a soft voice, promised that help would come soon.

A growing fear that Mooshie was suffering somewhere in this hell sent me to my feet. As I rose, a slight movement inside the closet caught my eye. From the top shelf, a pair of yellow-gold eyes gazed down at me.

"Mooshie?" I whispered. "Is that you?" A barely audible meow came in reply.

I stood on the chair, and using my thumbnail, scratched the caked dirt off the red plastic ID tag. I let out a cry and pulled the sable Burmese into my arms, holding him close. In the light from the window I saw that Mooshie was skin and bones, and his fur was matted and crawling with fleas.

Lola was still standing guard at the door when I fled the

house of horrors with Mooshie cradled in my arms. "Where's the nearest vet or animal hospital?" I asked, hurrying to the car.

In answer, Lola asked me to wait while she ran to her house. She returned a minute later with the directions to a nearby animal hospital.

"What are you going to do now?" she asked, handing me the slip of paper.

"First I'm going to get my cat to the vet, and then I'm going to file a report with the County Humane services and make sure the rest of those animals are removed and treated posthaste."

Lola pointed to the paper. "My name and phone number are on the back. Make sure you put me down as a witness. Neighbor or no neighbor, I'll testify if asked."

She stepped away from the car, her face full of worry.

"It's going to be okay, Lola," I said, praying I was right.

*

Within the hour Mooshie was being examined by a veterinarian who told me my cat was anemic and suffering from a respiratory infection. He was also malnourished and loaded with worms. For the next two days, Mooshie received intravenous antibiotics and nutritional supplements. He was treated for ear mites, dewormed, and given a series of flea baths.

With support from the veterinarian and her staff, I was directed to the County Humane Investigations office where I filed a formal complaint of animal neglect and cruelty against the Freddy Krueger of cat minders.

With Mooshie in good hands, I went back to my hotel and set about hunting down the best person I could think of to minister to my cat while he recuperated. It was a long shot, but I was going to try and find Harry the stethoscope jockey.

The last I'd heard, Harry had received his RN and was working as a traveling nurse in Oregon. I had no idea what agency he worked with, so I called the nurses who I thought might remember him from his clinical rotations in their units. I couldn't believe my luck when the fourth nurse I called told me he'd taken a permanent position in a pediatric clinic in Marin.

Happy at the prospect of being reunited with his feline buddy, Harry readily agreed to care for Mooshie for the remainder of my time in Los Angeles. By the time Mooshie was discharged, I figured I'd have just enough time to drive him back to Marin and return to Hollywood when filming resumed.

The officers from County Humane Investigations called two days later to report that they, along with law enforcement, had removed all the animals from the house. I then checked in with Lola who informed me that Mr. K had not yet returned.

Over the coming months that I was in communication with the Humane Investigations Department, the law enforcement officers, and Lola, I kept tabs on the case against Mr. K. The twisted reasons for why he came to be the way he was meant little to me. My only concern was that he would never, for the remainder of his life, be allowed to mistreat another animal.

The day the film wrapped I drove back to Marin for a joyous reunion with my cat. Harry and I were still trading Mooshie stories when my landlady came to deliver the news that her son had been accepted at Stanford, and I was going to be paying his tuition by way of a substantial rent increase.

I gave my notice on the spot.

*

I don't remember why I thought going to Chicago was a good idea. I hate the cold with a passion, and I am a staunch vegetarian—two perfectly solid reasons not to live in a place where it snowed and a vegetarian meal meant you got a carrot along with a slab of beef, pork, or lamb.

I suppose practicality played a hand in my decision. I needed a place to get back in the wordsmithing saddle and begin work on my fourth book, *Tending Lives*. Chicago seemed like a good place to do that since rents and living expenses were a fraction of what it cost to live in the Bay Area.

Mooshie had bounced back from his Freddy Krueger experience with all his personalities and sense of humor intact. Considering our more recent experiences, I reckoned that Chicago would be a safe and distraction-free place for us both.

Our spacious third-story walk-up apartment was situated over a gay sex shop on North Halsted Street. Unlike the other apartments we were shown, ours was flooded with an abundance of natural light that came through the windows overlooking North Halsted Street. Mooshie loved these windows and their wide sills that provided him with a comfortable cat perch while he surveilled the busy street below.

His various reactions to the street activities were amusing to watch. Pigeons landing on the window ledge drove him into a frenzy of batting the window and voicing his *keh keh keh* pre-attack warning. The sight of dogs on leashes brought on hissing and spitting. Big trucks terrified him, and loud motorcycles sent him running for the safety of my lap. His come-play-with-me call he reserved expressly for the crowds of noisy teenagers who walked by before and after school.

When he tired of the windowsill, he would drape himself, belly up, over the couch's overstuffed armrest and snag my sleeves or my braid while I typed. If I ignored him or moved out of claw range, he would slip, inch by inch, further over the armrest until the upper half of his body was dangling upside down, front legs over his head. In this position he would stare up at me until I picked him up or he slid to the floor.

All was copacetic while the sun still shone on Chicago, but when the sun went away and blizzards threatened to blow out our windows, things promptly tobogganed downhill.

A native of upstate New York, I was no stranger to ice storms, blizzards, or temperatures of minus twenty degrees. However, being familiar with those things didn't mean I liked them. Truth be told, as soon as skies turn gray and the temperature drops below seventy-two degrees, both my cat and I plunge into a state of abject misery.

To keep himself warm, Mooshie took to sleeping over the pilot light on top of the gas stove. One day the landlord came by unexpectedly to check on the apartment's thermostat. Recognizing the man's characteristic knock, I snatched Mooshie off the stove and threw him in the oven. (There was an unspoken "no pets" rule that I'd disregarded, rationalizing that Mooshie was more of a life coach than a pet.)

A lonely bachelor and a renowned talker, my landlord asked for a cup of tea. I made sure he sat in the chair that faced away from the stove so that I could sit facing it, keeping an eye on Mooshie.

With sad Margarete Keane-esque eyes, Mooshie watched me through the glass in the oven door while my landlord and I discussed the state of the Union and the latest display of whips, dildos, and ball gags in the shop window below.

The moment the landlord departed I opened the oven thinking Mooshie would be happy to get out. Instead, he fought me, insisting on spending the rest of the day sleeping on the warm oven floor. From then on, he rarely budged from that spot.

Despite the blizzards and ice storms, I refused to give up running. Each morning I pulled a waterproof snowsuit over three layers of clothes. I protected my running shoes inside four layers of plastic shopping bags secured with thick rubber bands around my ankles. It was in this restriction of clothing that I'd head over to Lincoln Park, crinkling with every step.

The bulky Pillsbury Doughboy getup and two pairs of

sub-zero gloves slowed me down enough that I had to take care when leaving the apartment, lest Mooshie escape while I negotiated the task of getting the door closed.

Mooshie's general refusal to move away from the warmth of his oven lulled me into a false sense of security. He must have been planning his escape for weeks, calculating precisely how long it took me to make my way out the door.

One below-freezing February morning as I fumbled with the door, Mooshie seized the opportunity to bolt from the oven, slip around the plastic bags that covered my feet, and make a run for it. With a sinking heart I watched him trot down the outside corridor that was presently covered with eight inches of freshly fallen snow. He'd gone about fifteen feet when the reality of minus-five degrees Fahrenheit, and snow deeper than he was tall, alerted his thermoreceptors that there was a profound temperature breach.

He came to an abrupt halt, stood on his hind legs, and glanced around in confusion. Leaping like a deer over the blanket of snow, he returned to his oven.

A few days after Mooshie's Great Snow Escape, he left his oven and took to sitting in one of the rear windows, staring out at the snow. He stopped chasing after his stuffed mice, and all purring ceased. It was clear that he was suffering from Feline Seasonal Affective Disorder.

Worried for his health, I was wracking my brains trying to think of where to head next when fate once again stepped in to save us.

*

The woman who called explained that she'd heard about me and my cat from a friend's yoga instructor, who told her that we were conscientious long-term property sitters. She went on to explain that she owned a home in sunny Ojai, California, and would we consider housesitting for six months while she went to Europe?

I gazed out the window while she spoke and watched the latest blizzard rage. The outside thermometer read minus eight.

"What's the temperature there right now?" I asked.

"It's seventy-four degrees," she replied. Then, as if she'd heard the howling wind and sleet slamming against our windows, she slyly added, "I'm sitting outside in my shorts and halter top."

I pulled my suitcase out of the closet and emptied the dresser drawers into it while we went over details and set a date for our arrival. By the time I hung up, I'd written and signed the intention to vacate notice for my landlord.

Two weeks later we were on our way to California.

*

Ojai was a city of contrasts. The rich and famous lived side by side with farmworkers and the crystal-gazing hippies the sixties left behind. Citrus farmers, pot growers, movie stars, artists, and municipal workers all attended the same cultural events and got along relatively well.

The house that was to be our home for the next six months was set behind an iron gate on twenty wooded acres near the Topatopa and Sulphur Mountains. The house was massive, not in the showy California look-at-me-I'm-rich way, but more in a modernist Getty-Museum-hidden-in-the-woods style.

A true design snob at heart, Mooshie loved it. Having six thousand square feet of luxurious space and scores of sunlight puddles to bask in kept him busy and content. It was a thrill to write with a panoramic view of a mountain range and seated at a desk that, according to the owner, once belonged to Emily Brontë.

We'd been in residence for about two weeks when Mooshie began pawing at the door, begging to be let outside. Being as we were in a densely wooded valley surrounded by mountains, I gave in to my cat's desires.

It was on one of those Southern California days when the air is filled with the scent of pitcher sage and oranges that I first let Mooshie out on his leash. He scampered around, sniffing every inch of ground before throwing himself down in the dirt and blissfully rolling side to side.

Each day he'd make his way to the same patch of earth and sing his come-play-with-me song, letting all creatures of the wilderness know he was available for a playdate.

I happened to glance out the window one day to see Mooshie's leash whipping back and forth, sending leaves flying in all directions. I stepped outside and found him playing tag-and-chase with a red fox pup.

Twenty years earlier I'd had a brief introduction to a domesticated red fox. My memory of the animal was that it behaved more like a feline than a canine, although technically, the opposite is true—or as a cat-loving tech-savvy friend of mine once quoted: "Foxes are cat software running on dog hardware."

Knowing there would be a vixen nearby, I grabbed my binoculars and spotted her about forty feet away in a cluster of rocks, her eyes fixed on her offspring.

Sensing she was being observed, she located me at once. As we regarded each other, I couldn't help but wonder if we were thinking the same thing—should we let the kids have their fun, or should we break it up? Taking the lead, the vixen sat down, and I returned to my desk to watch the two animals romp.

The pup showed up again a few days later. The two were well into their game when they suddenly stopped and began sniffing the air. Vulpine and feline ears pricked forward as their eyes fixed on the same point in the distance. Thinking a deer had drawn their attention, I was about to return to my work when the vixen came running and drove her pup away with nips and scolding barks. She passed the window where I sat and fixed me with a gaze that practically screamed: *DANGER, you twit!*

This time I heeded both my father's and Salem's wise counsel about trusting the instincts of the creatures that inhabited the natural world. Taking the vixen's urgency as my cue, I charged into the yard. Sure enough, the birds were silent, nothing was moving, and Mooshie was still focused on something in the distance. I turned up my senses and followed his line of sight to an outcrop not thirty yards away. There, blending in with the rocks, crouched a Puma concolor—also known as a cougar, catamount, panther, puma, and mountain lion.

Her eyes trained on my cat, she padded down from the rocks with all the grace of a ballerina. My first impulse was to reel my cat in by the leash, but I knew firsthand how fast a cougar could move. During my years of running remote trails in California, I'd had my fair share of up-close encounters with mountain lions.

I mentally reviewed the list of things one should do when having a head-on confrontation with a mountain lion. Turning to face the big cat full on, my eyes on hers, I inched closer to Mooshie, reciting the cardinal rule: never run from, turn your back on, or take your eyes off a mountain lion that has you in its sights.

The big cat regarded me for a moment, dismissed me as little or no threat, and picked up her pace. The fact that my presence in no way intimidated her added to my fear. Following the advice given by wilderness guides the world over on what to do to make a mountain lion back off, I got on my tiptoes, waved my arms over my head, and shouted at her to scram.

Not only did the mountain lion not back down, my threatening display only served to piss her off. She bared her teeth and kept right on coming. Briefly I wondered if the animal thought Mooshie was her cub.

The cougar's determination to get to my cat and her complete dismissal of me as any kind of serious threat triggered my deep-throated shriek. Oblivious to the danger he was in, at the same moment of my scream, Mooshie took a step *toward* the mountain lion and voiced his cheery three-tone invite: *Hey big mama! Come on over and give me a lick bath!*

It wasn't my outraged scream that slowed the big cat down, it was Mooshie's come-play-with-me invite. Confused by our conflicting messages, the mountain lion stopped in her tracks.

Never taking my eyes off her, I reached down, got my cat in an iron grip, unhooked his leash, and shoved him under my sweater as I began moving backwards in the direction of the house.

The mountain lion hissed and started for us again.

In my peripheral vision, I estimated that I was maybe fifteen feet from the door. I kept my eyes glued to hers while I continued taking backward steps, one step at a time.

I yelled again, hoping she would give up and run away now that my cat was out of sight.

Nope.

Instead, she snarled and rushed forward in a feigned attack, both front legs off the ground, claws out, and fangs showing.

In a loud even voice, I again told her to stay back. I then made the serious error of glancing away for a nanosecond to estimate the remaining distance to the door. My eyes returned to hers at the moment her hindquarters dipped and her powerful back legs tensed for the attack.

I jumped back and sideways, covering the remaining few feet to the door as the cougar sprang, her front legs open wide as if she were coming in for a flying hug.

Crying out in relief, I stumbled through the door that I'd left open in my haste. I glanced up in time to see the cougar's demeanor change from attack mode to surprise, and finally disgusted retreat.

I slammed the door shut with my foot. Still trembling, I pulled Mooshie out from under my sweater. His pupils were fully dilated, which I assumed had more to do with my rush of adrenaline than any self-protective instincts he may have had.

He pushed his head against my neck. I held onto him until our heart rates returned to normal. "What the bloody hell, Mooshie? You told that mountain lion that you wanted to be *friends*? Don't you recognize a killer cat when you see one?"

In response, he frantically began licking my face.

I held him at arms' length and said quietly: "I hate to say it pal, but your outside play dates in the Wild Kingdom have just come to an abrupt end."

Mooshie put his paw on my mouth—his way of telling me to shut up.

That night he came to sit on my desk. I paused in my work to study his elegant form as he sang his love song—a full-throated purr that soothed us both.

I leaned toward him and said quietly: "Someday, Mr. Mushu Pork With Pancakes, you're going to cause me to have a heart attack. You know that, right?"

My cat intoned a string of chirps that I interpreted as, *Yes, and your point is . . . ?*

"I just want you to know in advance that if I die from said heart attack, I'll still love you."

Wearing an expression of infinite compassion, Mooshie climbed onto my shoulder, nuzzled my ear, and wheezed his response: *As well you should, my devoted follower.*

·15·

LET THE GOOD TIMES ROLL ...
BUT WATCH OUT FOR THE GRAPES
OF WRATH

"Cats tell me without effort all that there is to know."

— Charles Bukowski, *On Cats*

There must have been a scarcity of conscientious long-term house sitters in America. Within days of the Ojai job ending, Mooshie and I again found ourselves on the road driving east to a three-month housesitting job in the Garden District of New Orleans.

It didn't take long to settle into the rhythm of The Big Easy. The balmy weather, the Creole cuisine, and the seductive southern charm all helped to put a love spell on me and my four-legged companion.

Mooshie took to the 1899 shotgun house immediately. His favorite place to hang out was on top of a peculiar seven-foot metal monolith that had inexplicably been placed in a corner of the main room. Even though this lofty perch wasn't the warmest spot in the house, he must have felt safe up there, because he rarely left it during the day except to eat, use his litterbox, and spend time with Sophie Marie.

*

The elderly woman who strolled by the house twice a day was a most intriguing figure. Invariably dressed in beautiful bright prints and matching headdress, she would often stop, shade her eyes, and gaze into our windows as if expecting to see someone she knew.

We'd been in residence about a week when Mooshie began settling on the front window sill moments before the woman showed up. The two would then stare at each other, neither one moving so much as an eyelash. A minute or two later the woman would nod and move on, talking to herself. Mooshie watched after her until she was out of sight, then returned to whatever he was about before she came by.

One morning we were lounging on the porch glider when a birdlike voice cut through the quiet of the day.

"Hey! You! *Ti fiy!* You! Girl! I want to see the cat."

I glanced up to see our daily stroll-by lady decked out in a brightly-colored flounced skirt and a blouse covered with beads of every color. On her head, she wore a scarlet taffeta turban that shimmered when it caught the light. Each finger bore a ring, and both wrists jangled with multiple bracelets. In direct contrast to all this high-color frippery were her silver skull earrings.

I rose from the glider to greet the woman. "Hello there! I've been meaning to—" Before I could utter another word, Mooshie sprang off the porch railing and ran to the woman with all the enthusiasm of a child greeting his beloved grandmother after a long absence.

The woman gathered him into her arms, speaking in rapid Creole.

Again pulling from my grammar school French, I was able to pick out enough words to understand the gist of what was being said.

"My sweet *bébé*! My little angel! I have found you!"

Somewhat perplexed, I paused. Did this woman think Mooshie was her lost cat?

I stepped forward and introduced myself, only slightly put off by the way Mooshie was contentedly purring in response to her honeyed affections. My cat pushed himself possessively into the woman's bosom and clung to her when I drew near. The woman gave me the once-over.

"I am Sophie Marie," she said, standing tall. "Louisiana Creole."

Unsure of the proper Creole etiquette, I curtsied and invited her in for tea.

This scene, minus the introductions and the curtsies, was to become a daily routine. It was soon clear that Sophie came to visit Mooshie and not me. I would be on one side of the kitchen table asking about the history of New Orleans while on the other side, Sophie would be cuddling with Mooshie. She would mumble brief answers to my questions then return her full attention to my cat.

If I left the room for any length of time, upon my return I invariably found the two conversing in what sounded like a feline version of Creole. Not a day went by that Sophie didn't make offers of money, love potions, and free spiritual purifications in exchange for Mooshie. As politely as possible, I refused all offers with the explanation that Mooshie and I were spiritual partners. From the way the woman narrowed her eyes, I surmised she wasn't buying it.

Perplexed by Sophie's obsession with Mooshie, I probed as delicately as possible about what she imagined her tie to him was. She never answered directly and would either change the subject or simply disregard me.

After a week of being brushed off, I finally held up my hands in surrender.

"Okay, I give up. I know Mooshie isn't your ordinary everyday housecat, but you act as if you know him. Does he remind you of a cat you lost, or maybe a cat you had as a child? Help me understand what connection you believe you have with my cat."

Instead of answering, Sophie whispered in Mooshie's ear and put him down. He looked to her as if asking for further instruction. Speaking in French, she told him to have a nap on the red chair in the front room. Mooshie obediently trotted to the red chair and settled in for a nap.

I disregarded the goosebumps on my arms and faced her. "Explain," I croaked.

"The *minou* called to me," Sophie said. "He is *mon ange gardien* like what do you say a, um—"

"He's your guardian angel?"

"*Oui*. He called me here. How else would I know where to look? I saw him and I knew he is Lisette."

"Lisette? Is that your lost cat? Mooshie is a male cat so he can't be—"

"*Non!*" Sophie slapped her hand on the table and got to her feet. "You do not understand! You insult me!"

"I am not insulting you, Sophie, and I *am* trying to understand. Please, sit down. I would like to hear about Lisette."

Reluctantly, the woman sat and collected herself. "Lisette was my baby daughter. She took sick with the pneumonia."

I touched her hand. "Oh, I am sorry, Sophie."

Sophie looked into her lap. "She passed during the Civil War."

I kept my expression neutral. "Your infant daughter died during the Civil War?"

Sophie nodded.

"Was this in a past life?"

She frowned. "Of course! How else?"

"And you think Mooshie is your baby's reincarnation?"

"I do not think, I *know!* The little *minou* is my baby daughter. She wants her *maman*. You see the way she loves Sophie? There can be no doubt."

A hundred possible replies zipped through my head, but I resolved to keep it simple.

"Lisette may very well want her mommy, Sophie, but you cannot have my cat. From the way Mooshie expects me to wait on him, I'm pretty sure he was my husband in *our* last

240

lives, so we have some past karma to work through."

The woman looked so heartbroken, I put my arm around her frail shoulders.

"You know, Sophie, I've been thinking. I'd like to spend a whole day and evening exploring the French Quarter, but I'd rather not leave Mooshie alone that long. Would you like to hang out with him while I'm gone?"

Sophie clapped her hands and agreed at once.

The doorbell rang at the stroke of eight the following morning. I swung open the door and was briefly dazzled into silence.

Crowned by an exquisite headdress of beads, crystals, and feathers, Sophie was further adorned with at least five pounds of costume jewelry and attired in a gorgeous multicolored dress.

Upon seeing the old woman, Mooshie rolled around the floor and jumped from one piece of furniture to the other like a bedeviled lunatic. The last time he'd been so animated was when he was a juvenile felinquent and off his leash.

Only when Sophie pushed past me did I notice the oversized duffle bag on wheels that she pulled behind her. I experienced a twinge of panic, worried that she might have interpreted "hang out" as "move in." But, I supposed, she was older and had certain requirements—a change of headwear and jewelry for the evening perhaps?

I decided the best way to address my concern was not to ask.

Mooshie jumped onto the duffel bag, clawing the canvas with purpose. I again wondered what might be in there and if it was alive, but dismissed the horrifying thoughts and looked the other way.

I slipped out the door, glancing back only long enough to see Sophie roll up her sleeves, throw her head back, and yell, "*Laissez les bons temps rouler!*" Let the good times roll!

On my way to the St. Charles streetcar line, I began to worry. Was Sophie desperate enough to catnap Mooshie? Or would I have a stroke and drop dead due to pins being stuck into a doll made in my likeness?

I shook myself back into reality and boarded the streetcar. Stroke or no stroke, I was determined to enjoy every minute of my time in the French Quarter. By the time I stepped onto Bourbon Street, I was humming *Laissez Les Bon Temps Rouler*.

It was after midnight when I tiptoed up the front steps. The first thing I noticed was the silence. The second thing that got my attention was the odor of burning candles coming through the screen door.

Hand on the doorknob, I paused to consider all the things I might see upon entering the house. I slowly opened the door, mouth agape at the scene before me.

Inside a circle of candles, Mooshie and Sophie sat on the floor facing each other while flickering shadows danced over the walls and ceiling. On the floor between them were two incense burners and bowls of various grains and spices. Drawings of unfamiliar symbols were carefully placed around each bowl.

A silver replica of one of the symbols hung as a charm from Mooshie's collar. On closer inspection, I was alarmed to see that my cat was drooling.

"Hello?" I whispered from outside the circle.

Neither of them so much as blinked. It was as if the animal and the woman were made of wood. I lifted my foot to step inside the circle but Sophie wagged a finger and hissed.

I retreated to the kitchen, found a clear line of sight into the living room, and opened a can of tuna.

One of Mooshie's ears twitched.

I blew over the open can in his direction.

My cat lifted his head and sniffed.

"Attaboy!" I said and dumped the tuna into a shallow bowl.

My cat's eyes shifted to the kitchen.

"Come on, Moosh," I urged. "Break the spell. Come and get it." For emphasis, I gave the cat smack snacks can a shake.

Unable to hold back any longer, Mooshie issued a joyful chirp, vaulted over the candle barrier, and galloped at full speed toward the tuna, the metal charm scraping the floor as he went. He skidded to the bowl and plunged his face into the tuna.

Indignant, Sophie came to her feet, hands on hips. "*Tu es un traître, minou!*" she scolded as she snuffed out the candles and returned the ceremonial paraphernalia to the duffel bag.

She remained silent during the drive to her house, but before she got out of the car, I touched her arm. "Don't be too hard on him, Sophie. It's not so much that he is a traitor, it's more that he worships tuna above all else." I hesitated then added, "Nice try, though."

The next time Sophie came by, we were packing the car to head back to California. The moment Mooshie saw her, he leaped into her arms. A forgiving soul, Sophie kissed his head and graciously presented him with a can of tuna and a vintage silver baby rattle inscribed with the name Lisette.

*

That summer we housesat for three months in Marin. When the job ended, I got the notion to rent a house in Paso Robles—a halfway point between the two planets of Northern and Southern California. The realtor I'd spoken with on the phone described the rental as, "a beautiful rustic cottage in an idyllic orchard of almond trees." It was, she assured me, the perfect place for a writer and her cat.

We arrived in Paso Robles two weeks later. I drove down the dirt road that bordered the property, searching for the so-called idyllic orchard. What I found instead was row upon row of almond trees that had died a couple of decades, if not centuries ago.

A sudden strong wind came up and turned the whole landscape into an impromptu reenactment of a California Dust Bowl documentary. Milling around a cluster of dilapidated trailers were ten or so rawboned men who looked like they were straight out of central casting for *The Grapes of Wrath*. Judging by the psychedelic, pornographic graffiti that decorated each caravan and the pungent smell of hashish, I guessed the encampment had been established sometime during the counterculture revolution of the sixties.

Kitty-corner from the trailers was the "beautiful rustic cottage," a tumbledown shack with a flat, tarpaper roof that, at the moment, held two mangy goats. Another six goats and a dozen sickly chickens sporting some serious ringworm were gathered in front of the hovel like a downtrodden welcoming committee.

I stole another glance at the Dust Bowl men who were now showing undisguised interest in what might be inside the car. Not daring to leave Mooshie alone, I tucked him under my arm, locked the car, and briskly made my way through the piles of empty beer cans to the shack. I pushed the goats aside and entered the two-room dump.

A powerful smell of sewage hit us head-on. From the way Mooshie was squirming to get away, I surmised he was having a flashback to his experience at Mr. K's. Still, a perverse curiosity drove me forward. Holding my breath, I stepped into the main room.

The wall-to-wall carpet was badly stained with swaths of what might have been motor oil. More disturbing was the cluster of weeds which had grown through a worn spot. The water-stained wallpaper, circa 1949, hung in strips.

I turned, ready to run, but it was too late. Like something out of a horror movie, clouds of what I took to be coarse dust rose out of the carpet and surrounded us. Mooshie, quicker and smarter than I, squirmed and scratched, desperate to escape. Rivetted, I couldn't take my eyes off the rug, which seemed to be undulating. Thinking my eyes were playing tricks, I leaned down for a better look.

Swarms of fleas covered my legs and feet. A second

more, and they were on my arms and shirt. I fled, frantically searching for a water spigot. Mercifully, I found one with an attached hose and rigorously sprayed both of us down, head to toe.

The Dust Bowl refugees laughed uproariously, whooping and slapping their thighs. One lanky bare-chested man shouted, "Girl, you go on back and tell them damned real estate people to quit sendin' regular normal folk out here!"

Bristling at this remark, I drove directly to the nearest hotel, where I showered and then ran a hot bath for the both of us to soak away any remaining fleas. Half in and half out of the water, Mooshie rested languidly on my chest, playing with the bath bubbles while I worked cat shampoo into his fur.

"Damn it Moosh, how dare that guy call us regular normal folks! You don't think we're regular normal folks, do you?"

Bubbles clinging to his whiskers, Mooshie shook the suds out of his ears wearing an expression that said, *Hell no. Why be normal?*

I kissed the top of my cat's head and smiled. "Good boy. I couldn't have said it better myself."

*

Mooshie and I fell into the habit of housesitting for four months every summer in Marin and renting the Fishermen Flats place in Florida for the rest of the year.

I sold the LeMans when the price of gas began to rise without letup. Getting ten miles to the gallon wasn't sensible when one was driving across the country twice a year. I purchased a Honda FE which got fantastic gas mileage, but Mooshie hated it, so I signed it over to Simon. I then bought the car I thought my cat would like the most—a used Plymouth minivan.

To give him plenty of roaming room I removed both rear bench seats. And since authors are always on the lookout for new material, I installed a CB radio so I could listen in on truck drivers' conversations—you never knew when a few good truck driver stories might come in handy.

Each September I'd pack the minivan with cat food, cat toys, kitty litter, and plenty of cat smack snacks. For myself, I brought a thermos for hot tea, a good supply of audiobooks, homemade hummus, and raw veggies.

We drove through death-defying sandstorms, hailstorms, rainstorms, and one-hundred-and-twenty-degree heat, building nerves of steel as we went. During the years we made this biannual 3500-mile journey, Mooshie and I came to know some of the worst drivers to infect American highways. Whenever I dared to look at my fellow drivers in the rearview mirror, they all wore the same maniacal expression as Punxsutawney "Don't Drive Angry" Phil while he drove the getaway truck in *Groundhog Day.*

Mooshie helped keep my stress levels low by the hilarious way he treated our fellow road warriors. Bored with prowling for random cat snacks, my cat would climb atop our luggage under the rear window and use his yellow bug-eyes to stare down the drivers behind us. This had the effect of both repelling and attracting tailgaters. I'd see drivers and their passengers either laughing and pointing or making the sign of the cross before dropping back.

We learned many things driving across America. For example, if I ever become suicidal, I know that all I need to do is drive around Philadelphia at the posted speed limit.

Mooshie was not particularly fond of staying in motels or hotels, although he did seem enraptured by the wide variety of smells he found on all those icky sticky carpets. The first thing he did when we checked into a room was to spend an hour observing things from under the bed. When he was ready, he would crawl out and start sniffing the rug. Occasionally, he'd zero in on some spot in the carpeting and start pawing at it, trying to cover it up. Finished with his smell fest, he'd jump on the bed and give his paws a meticulous cleaning. Watching him do this night after night ensured that I would never again go barefoot in a motel or hotel room, no matter how many stars they rated.

Mooshie was skilled at finding ingenious hiding places in these rooms for hire. Much too smart to go for the obvious places like under the pillows or inside the bed frame, my cat sought out hidey-holes that one needed a private investigator's skills to track down.

Harry Houdini had nothing on my cat. I mean, who would think to look for a cat compressed between the hanging ironing board and the closet wall? Inside the air conditioner casing? Pressed against the back wall of the room safe? Or how about sitting on the toilet tank, obscured between two halves of a hanging towel?

I could easily see Mooshie passing on these clever

concealment techniques in a how-to booklet for antisocial cats entitled, *Mooshie's Travel Tips for the Tricky Kitty: Hiding Up, Under, and In Between.*

The point where armadillos and alligators replaced raccoons and jackrabbits as the primary roadkill was a sure indication that we were in the south.

When we were five miles from Fishermen Flats, Mooshie would stop fussing and begin sniffing. Undoubtedly, he could smell the Gulf of Mexico and knew that not only was the torment nearly over, but he was about to receive the treat he'd been waiting for since we left California—a bucket of Kentucky Fried Chicken.

KFC was a mile from the drawbridge that led to our barrier island. Parking where he could watch me like a hawk, I'd purchase a three-piece bucket of whisker lickin' good chicken—hold the coleslaw, the mashed potatoes with gravy, the biscuit, the drink, and the chocolate chip cookie, please.

As I approached the van, bucket in hand, I could see Mooshie through the side windows standing on his hind legs, his whiskers twitching with excitement. The second the bucket touched the car floor, he'd dive in head first, devouring the chicken tenders, fried batter and all.

On our return to Marin in June, we had a similar ritual, except instead of being rewarded with KFC, Mooshie was treated to a Jack in the Box fish sandwich. He'd tear apart the bun, swat the lettuce and tomato off onto the floor, drag the pickle slices to one side, then sink his teeth into that slab of crusty deep-fried pollock smothered in tartar sauce.

The pickle slices he saved for last. Sneaking up on them, he'd fiercely shake each one, as if to shake the salty insolence out of it. Assured they couldn't retaliate, he'd then chew a slice, working it over like a toothless old man gumming a handful of potato chips. There was something about the salt or the sour pickling brine that would make him drool, but it never stopped him from eating every slice.

On what would be his last return trip to Marin, I remember watching Mooshie killing the pickles and thinking how far he'd come from our first cross-country trip when he stood on the passenger seat with his front paws on the dashboard, and eyes fixed on the road like an anxious DMV driving test examiner.

Once he was assured that my driving abilities could be trusted, he slowly evolved into a seasoned traveler and trusty co-pilot. This might be pushing it, but I believe Mooshie relished having his own personal chauffeur and event planner.

Still, I don't think he missed being on the road, because he sailed into our next phase of life without a hitch.

PART FIVE

RETIREMENT:
A BLANKET OF ONE'S OWN

·16·

LOOK WHAT THE CAT DRAGGED IN

"If you want to write, keep cats."
— Aldous Huxley *(1895 – 1963)*

When it comes to writing fiction, I am not a speedy writer. It takes me a long time to develop a plot and outline the story. The characters must be created, each with his or her unique history, personality, motivations, and flaws. Then there are the necessary twists and turns and red herrings that add flavor and spice to the mix.

Once the storyboard is completed and pinned to the wall, all that is left to do is sit down and write the book or, as was in my case, books.

In 1995 Random House offered me a mystery series contract—delivering one book every six months. Let me be clear—the very *thought* of having to meet such tight deadlines in a genre I had no experience with sent me on a wild ride into the private hell of Ultimate Writer's Performance Anxiety.

Nevertheless, I still needed to buy groceries and pay rent, not to mention the mounting vet bills for Mooshie's increasing bouts of the Mystery Plague. The intravenous amoxicillin that marginally curbed his symptoms enough to get him back on his paws required hospitalization, which meant substantial contributions to the veterinarian's vacation home mortgage fund.

When I signed the Random House contract, I knew it was time to quit our nomadic adventures. Mooshie was slowing down. He needed a rest from the rigors of being on the move, and I needed to put my nose to the grindstone and get those mysteries written.

The question was *where* to settle. The thing that finally motivated me to give up on the idea of settling in Marin came the day I checked out a rental in a quiet rural town at the west end of the county. The ad read:

```
Charming one-room cottage in woodsy
West Marin. $650/mo. Applications
will be accepted at the showing on
Sunday 1 to 4 p.m.
```

Marin rents were absurdly overblown, so six hundred and fifty dollars seemed too reasonable to be true. But since rentals were scarce, I figured it was worth a look.

On the appointed day I kissed my cat good-bye and made my way west. I was early, but as I turned onto the narrow road a mile from the address, I found myself in a line of cars. Thinking there must be a town event of some kind, I continued creeping forward until it occurred to me that the cars were all heading to the "charming cottage." I parked a half-mile away and walked to the address, where I was surprised to find a sweet, well-maintained cottage behind a picket fence.

Due to the substantial turnout, the landlord took only ten people in at a time to see the rental. The rest of us were asked to wait in front. When it was my group's turn, we were ushered into the cottage . . . and straight out the backdoor. We were then led to a fifteen-by-twelve-foot garden shed-type structure at the far end of the yard.

The first thing I noticed when I stepped inside was the bare plywood floor. The elements of drywall and electrical outlets were conspicuously absent. In place of electrical outlets were two orange heavy-gauge extension cords that had been pushed up through holes in the floor, one at each end of the room. Against the wall, still in their boxes, were a space heater, a double burner hot plate, and two multi-outlet surge protectors.

We were then shown a closet that contained a toilet and sink. Overhead, a garden hose with a spray nozzle attached to the end dangled from a hole in the ceiling. The caulking used to hold the hose in place was still wet.

When the prospective landlord pointed out the cheap stainless-steel drain cover over a hole in the floor and called it a "special feature," I became apoplectic, not so much by the absurdity (not to mention the illegality) of the place, but because the other applicants were bidding up the rent on a silent auction form that hung from a tack by the door.

I hotfooted it to my car. On the way back to central Marin I pulled over at the first payphone I saw and called the owner of Fishermen Flats. The flat, he told me, was not available, but he did have a small fishing cottage on the water that was currently for rent.

I leased it with an option to rent for a second, and possibly a third year.

*

The fishing cottage was everything I could have dreamed of in a charming tropical writer's nook. Situated on a narrow spit of land that lay between Palma Sola Bay and the Gulf of Mexico, the distance between the two bodies of water could be walked in under sixty seconds. We had our own dock, a sun porch, and a small yard. There were hardwood floors, lots of windows, and a refreshing cross breeze between the two bodies of water.

We quickly settled in—I to write obsessively, and Mooshie to veg out on the sunporch watching the dolphins and manatee that routinely visited our dock.

Mooshie's reaction to the marine mammals was a see-saw display of feline fascination and indifference. Each time one would surface to take a breath, my cat would crouch, his whiskers twitching. The moment the marine mammal submerged, Mooshie would return to his normal activity of dozing while he waited for the next surfacing.

As for the mysteries, I limped along, learning as I went. I'm not sure why, but Mooshie was especially clingy during the first few months in our new cottage. He took to sitting behind my monitor, his eyes just clearing the top. He would then stare at me without blinking for as long as I could stand it; usually about thirty minutes.

If I still managed to ignore him, he'd work his way around the monitor an inch at a time, step over my keyboard, wedge himself in between my forearms, and rest his nose on my chin.

Nighttime was especially difficult for him. Each night around ten, he would rouse himself from wherever he was, hop onto my desk, and let his eyes bore into the side of my head. If I didn't react, he'd crank up the volume on his high-pitched nasal squeak. When that annoying ploy didn't stop my fingers from working over the keyboard, he'd reach up, snag the temple hinge of my glasses, pull them off my face, and gnaw on the silicone nose pads.

This would go on until I lost my train of thought along with my patience. I would then pick him up and hold him so that we were eye to eye. "What do you want from me?"

He'd cock his head and chirp out his complaint: *Do you have any idea what time it is?*

I'd roll my eyes, put my glasses back on, and continue writing.

He'd then crawl into my lap and make his annoyance felt by tapping my nose or my mouth with his open paw so that his claws barely scraped the skin. All this did was earn him a return trip to the floor. Undaunted, he'd jump back into the saddle and repeat this behavior ten or more times until his legs got tired.

His next stratagem was to jump up and drape himself

over my left shoulder. If I kept on typing, he'd inch his body down my back until his front paws reached the top edge of my office chair. He would then rest his rear end against the side of my face—level with my nose.

If I pushed him away from my face, he would then commence whipping his tail back and forth across the front of my glasses. I'd ignore this aggravation until he knocked them off. After being returned to the floor, he would sit at my feet and stare up at me, making mewing sounds with a broken-hearted whine at the end.

His sorry mewing didn't fool me. Within a minute or two he'd move on to another annoying behavior, like getting a solid hold on one of my feet and chewing on my toenails.

If I yielded to his demands, he'd wait while I shut down the computer and then watch my every move as I brushed my teeth, washed my face, and put on my pajamas. He was always fascinated by this routine—as if he hadn't seen me do these things a thousand times before. Once I was in bed, he'd jump up on my chest and rest his nose on my lips for a kiss. He would then curl up between my neck and shoulder and begin chattering and chirping as if giving me a recap of his day.

Should I even try to read, he would either climb over the top of the book and sit on it or climb under it and plop himself on my face while kicking the book off the bed with his hind legs.

If I refused to give in to his demands that I retire for the night, he would seek refuge with Mother Teresa, who had entered Mooshie's life in the form of a blanket.

I don't remember from which garage sale or thrift shop I'd purchased the blanket, but the second Mooshie laid eyes on it, he claimed it as his. Made of soft, knobby cotton, the blanket was white and edged with blue stripes the exact hue and pattern as Mother Teresa's sari. Each time he did battle with the Mystery Plague, Mother Teresa was always there to provide him with a secure sickbed nest. It was Mooshie's security blanket and his favorite place to rest while he waited for the boozers to show up.

Up the street and around the corner was a down-home beer-and-Old Crow kind of bar that was originally owned by Babe Ruth in 1930. At two a.m. the tourists were driven out, but a few of the regular inebriates—historical landmarks in and of themselves—were allowed to stay on.

Around seven each evening Mooshie would be on his Mother Teresa blanket, and I'd be sitting on the sunporch writing when this same small band of professional alcoholics would stroll past our cottage on their way to the bar. And, we'd still be there some eight and a half hours later when they stumbled past us on their way home.

For reasons unknown, one perpetually blitzed born-again redneck was offended by the fact I worked long hours. One night she scratched on the sunporch screen and slurred, "What the hell is wrong with you?! You never move from that damned chair. You're locked up tighter than an unopened can of okra! Go have a goddamned drink and loosen up! And that goes for the goddamned cat, too!"

Fascinated by the raucous tipplers, Mooshie jumped up

on the windowsill and studied the intoxicated woman and her soused companions with quiet compassion. An extended silence fell as the feline Buddha and the hammered humans regarded one another.

One or two minutes into this visual meditation, my cat yawned, gave his audience a few chirps of advice about the benefits of sobriety, and returned to Mother Teresa.

Mollified by Mooshie's chirps of wisdom, the blitzed crowd staggered on.

*

Mooshie was enamored of books, except his love for them came in the form of tearing into them, and sometimes devouring them—depending on the quality of the paper.

Everyone owns at least one dog-eared book, right? Every book *I* owned was cat-nibbled. If I left a book where he could get to it, Mooshie would manage to get it open, lie on top of it, and beginning at the corner of one page, systematically bite through the paper. He'd pull off a corner, shake it to make sure it was truly dead, then move on to the next page. By the time he finished the book, he'd created a pile of ripped page corners—like so many raked up literary leaves.

If there was even the slightest bit of grease or food smudge on a page, he'd sniff it, lick it, tear it off, and eat it. Other times he'd just puncture each page so that the book looked like someone went after it with a tiny hole punch.

I always kept a copy of *The Random House Dictionary of the English Language* next to my computer. Out of the blue one day, Mooshie decided the mammoth tome was the greatest thing since can openers. It provided him a lofty perch from which he kept surveillance on the yard and the deck. When he grew bored with monitoring his surroundings, he would study the miniscule print with great interest, drooling on any illustration that took his fancy, or resting his paw over a word he particularly liked.

Every time I tried to move him off the book in order to check a word, he'd fight the hand that pushed him. As soon as his rump hit the desk, he'd try to crawl back onto the page. I'd be searching for the word I wanted with my left hand, while my right hand fought off the feline book hog.

The reason for his intense desire to sit atop the book wasn't clear until the thing under the cottage revealed itself.

During one of his remissions from the Mystery Plague, Mooshie was sitting atop the dictionary when his ears and chin commenced quivering. Voicing loud meows, he slid off the tome, down the leg of the table, and made for the screen door. I searched for the object of his attention, but other than a dolphin surfacing at the end of our dock, there was nothing to be seen.

A week later, strange sounds could be heard coming from under the cottage. I didn't give it much thought until Mooshie, nose pressed to the floor, circled one particular spot and settled down to sleep. For the next two weeks he refused to sleep anywhere else.

I returned from my run one morning to find my cat clinging to the top of the screen door, sniffing the air. He gave the safety chain a fond look, and for a moment I thought I saw the old desire for the thrill of a little asphyxiation creep into his eyes. Prying his claws off the screen, I let him outside.

Like a human on urgent business, he darted under the cottage.

I experienced a flash of panic. What if there was a twenty-foot Burmese (no relation) Python under there? Florida was rife with this species which favored sheltering under houses—especially houses near the water.

Worse, what if it was a nest of raccoons? I'd face off with a python any day before I'd go near a wild raccoon. Even though I grew up in a home where the family pet was a fully domesticated raccoon who used the toilet, washed his hands, and ate at the dining room table with us, I didn't much trust them in the wild, and I sure as hell didn't trust them with my cat.

I dropped to my knees and let my eyes adjust to the dark underbelly of the cottage. My cat sat near a low, dark pile of something I couldn't quite make out. At first I thought it might have been an old sweatshirt, or maybe a jacket—our boozers were always losing their shoes and various other articles of clothing. Mooshie once dragged a pair of abandoned boxer shorts into the cottage, then sat in front of me with them hanging from his snaggletooth. I tried to get them away from him, but he growled and set to rolling around on them in the same frenzied manner as when he was out of his mind on catnip.

The area where Mooshie was sitting was directly under the spot he'd been sleeping on inside the cottage.

Considering that he'd smelled whatever this thing was through the flooring, I wasn't sure it was something I wanted to see. At the same time, my curiosity refused to let me go back to work until I knew what the thing was.

I crawled in as far as I could before the pilings made it impossible to proceed farther. The only odor I detected was moist dirt. Keeping his eyes on the mound, Mooshie gave it a few whacks with his power paw.

The mound stirred.

He thumped the thing again with a rapid repeat motion. The dark lump began to rise. An image of Ratzilla flashed through my mind. Faster than I could give voice to the curse word on my tongue, I retreated, scraping my knees and bumping my head as I went. Before I could get all the way out, faint sounds of pitiful mewing reached my ears.

I automatically changed course and crawled forward again. Four kittens: two black and whites, one orange, and a muddy calico runt blindly separated from the pile and wobbled in my direction.

Ten feet away, a tortoiseshell feline with a stunning face divided precisely in half—one side orange, and the other, black—sat calmly watching us.

The mystery of my cat's desire to sit on top of the dictionary was solved—from that vantage point, Mooshie had been able to watch the mother cat's comings and goings from under the house.

After I set out water and a dish of ground raw chicken on the porch, Mooshie and I sat inside by the screen door, patiently waiting for the tortie to take the bait. It wasn't but a few minutes before she was wolfing down the chicken while Mooshie chirped. Her meal was cut short when an orange fuzzball the size of a softball tottered into the yard, mewling.

The tortie hurried over to the kitten and picking him up by the scruff, disappeared under the house.

Mooshie paced in front of the door then stood on his hind legs and pawed at the handle, his signal that he wanted to be let out.

When I didn't respond, he gave me a worried look.

"Don't worry," I said, picking him up for a reassuring cuddle. "She'll be back."

And come back she did. Because of her husky rasp of a voice, I named the tortie Joplin, after Janice Joplin. And though she never braved coming inside the cottage, the tortie was on the front porch first thing each morning, her brood in tow, crying for their breakfast.

Mooshie would wait patiently until they'd eaten before venturing out to sit next to Joplin. Content, they watched the kittens chase lizards and each other around the yard.

The kittens were about two months old when I trapped mom and brought her in for spaying and vaccinations. While Joplin was busy at the vet's, I brought the kittens to the local no-kill shelter for vaccinations and adoption.

Since feral cats her age would not be adoptable, I brought Joplin home and released her in the yard, fully expecting her to take off in search of her progeny. Instead, she ambled over to the porch and settled in for a long nap in the sun. She'd done her best as a mother, but I don't think she ever gave her brood or their absence a second thought after that.

Mooshie, Joplin, and I fell into a comfortable routine that I believe provided each of us with a sense of security. It was during this peaceful lull that I received a call from my next-door neighbor Kellie, the local shelter's principal vet tech.

She explained that the shelter was in the grip of a kennel cough epidemic, and would I be interested in fostering a few eight-week-old kittens until the respiratory illness was contained?

I described the situation to Mooshie and Joplin, acting out the stages of kennel cough: the kittens' pitiful mewling, coughing, and finally, pretending to fall dead. I then asked if they would like some company for a while.

The two cats looked at me blankly, which I took as their agreement that it would be a nice thing to do. Given how Mooshie fostered Joplin's litter, I resolved that if my cat could do it, so could I.

Kellie met me at the door of the shelter with two pet carriers which she insisted she load into the van herself. I managed to get a quick glimpse of gray fur and green eyes before she could obscure my view with the four cardboard boxes filled with tins of kitten food, four litter pans, and six five-pound bags of litter that followed.

As I was driving away, Kellie waved and told me to call if I ran out of food or cat litter. Thinking she was making a joke, I laughed. I mean, how much litter and food could three or four kittens go through in a week or two?

Back at the cottage I unloaded the supplies and brought in the carriers, alarmed by the weight of them. "Whoa!" I said as I lowered them onto my bed. "These must be some fat cats."

Mooshie sat at the foot of the bed, his eyes glued to the carriers.

"You have to be nice to our foster kitties," I said. "No playing rough or terrorizing them, okay?"

My cat chirped and threw me an impatient look that said, *What are you waiting for? Let them out before my curiosity kills another one of my lives.*

I opened both carrier doors at the same time. For a few seconds, nothing happened. A moment later, a gray face poked out of one cage, and a black face out of the other. Two diminutive noses sniffed the air and then, like a faucet turned to full, a gush of kittens—ten in all—spilled out onto the bed.

The mass of furballs rushed Mooshie—sniffing, hissing, leaping, and rolling about like enchanted marbles. My cat watched in either fascination, or indignation—it was hard to tell. A few minutes after the initial stampede, he relaxed and let them do to him as they pleased.

Mooshie was the best foster parent the kittens could have wished for. He played with them, taught them how to use the litterbox, and marshaled the food bowls to make sure they all got equal shares. Any kitten who tried to monopolize more than his share, Mooshie nudged aside and pushed the shy ones into place.

Joplin wanted nothing to do with the cluster of

interlopers. I invited her inside, but she always refused, preferring instead to sit outside the screen door and hiss whenever the kittens came near.

The day the shelter was deemed free of kennel cough, Kellie came by to collect our portion of the mob. Mooshie was sad to see them go, but his mood was soon bolstered when Kellie picked him up and praised him for being so good. By the time she presented him with a small package of cat smack snacks, he was purring.

In Andrew Vachss's *Safe House*, the question is asked, "When's the last time you saw a seeing-eye cat?" I suppose this was meant to play up cats' selfish nature. Mooshie did not conform to that particular stereotype for cats. I'm sure that had it been possible, he would have gladly taken on the duty of being a certified foster cat for every homeless kitten in the county.

*

Things went along smoothly for the next six months. Mooshie remained healthy, and with the help of my characters, the mysteries were progressing on schedule. In May of that year, I was asked to appear at several book events taking place in upstate New York and Boston. Given that I would be staying with my dad, he requested that I bring Mooshie along so they could keep each other company while I made my appearances.

I'd arranged to have Mooshie in coach with me, but when I arrived at the airport, I found that there had been a mix-up with pet reservations. Two cats were already booked on the flight, the limit for pets in coach. The next flight into Albany wasn't until the following morning at the same time I was scheduled for a television interview.

This left only one option—Mooshie would have to go in the cargo hold.

I balked, but then remembered Dr. Petrie telling me that it wasn't usually a problem for cats to fly in the cargo hold as long as the flight was less than four hours and the weather was fair. Our flight to Albany, with one quick stop in New Jersey, was less than four hours. It being May, the weather was mild.

A special cargo handler came to collect my cat, and the launch was all systems go. From my window seat, I watched two baggage handlers load luggage onto the conveyor belt. When the handler pulled Mooshie's carrier off the cart, my cat's front legs shot through the air holes. I imagined Mooshie yelling, *Hey! What the hell is this? This can't be right. Get me outta here!*

The second handler took the carrier from his coworker and peered inside. Mooshie took a swipe at his nose, which set both men off laughing. The first handler studied the ticket tied to the carrier and, not wanting to be left out of the fun, decided to offer his face for mauling too. Mooshie obliged the man by snagging his lower lip with an outstretched claw.

I groaned and looked away.

With the wind on our side, we landed in Albany ahead of schedule. I stayed in my seat, watching the baggage being unloaded. The carrier was nowhere to be seen.

I felt a brief ripple of concern but reassured myself that the carrier would have been placed in the pressurized and temperature-controlled section of the hold and would probably be unloaded last.

At the baggage carousel, I awaited the delivery of the carrier. After an hour and a half, my worst fear was confirmed—the carrier was nowhere to be found. When I asked the baggage service agent where the carrier might be, he thought about it for a while then replied, "Could be just about anywhere in the United States."

So much for reassurances.

The baggage service office encouraged me to go home and wait while the airlines hunted Mooshie down.

I couldn't stop worrying. Even my father's hilarious survival stories about growing up in a sizable Italian family failed to distract me. After my dad had retired for the night, I walked down to the Mohawk River. Sitting on the bank watching the water flow by, I made promises and deals with gods, saints, and dead relatives to please protect my cat and return him to me.

The following day I did one TV appearance, two radio shows, and a book signing. My mind was so tangled in the barbed wire of anxiety over my cat, how I got through them is a mystery. Had Mooshie been found? Was he dying of dehydration? What if the Mystery Plague hit him again? What if he'd been rerouted to someplace like Alaska where he'd freeze to death? Worse, what if he'd ended up in some extreme Bible Belt airport where dark brown or black cats with Chinese food names were thought of as demons?

I drove back to the airport and spent the rest of the evening in the company of the baggage service employees. One of the agents, an older woman who confided that she was owned by two cats, let me sit in a corner of the back office while she made multiple calls, trying to follow the carrier's trail.

She hung up, heaved a sigh, and ran her fingers through her hair. "I've got good news and bad news."

I closed my eyes. "Good news, first."

"The carrier was mistakenly unloaded during the flight's layover in New Jersey."

"And the bad news?"

"New Jersey hasn't been able to locate it."

"Is it possible the carrier was mistakenly loaded onto the luggage belt and someone picked it up?"

The agent shrugged. "Sure, but if that was true, why haven't they returned it yet?"

I wondered what kind of person would keep a cat that belonged to someone else, then remembered what a charming animal Mooshie was, and wondered who *wouldn't* want to keep him. Even people who didn't like cats, liked Mooshie.

I went home and worried myself to sleep.

The next morning, I received a call from the baggage office. The cat carrier had been located at the Trenton-Mercer Airport and was on its way back to Albany. I didn't ask if my cat was still alive, or if he was even in the carrier, and they didn't offer any further information.

My father drove me to the airport. The moment his back

bumper passed through the parking lot gate, I sprang out of the car and took off like an Olympic sprinter for the baggage claim office.

I detected an unmistakable undercurrent of tension the moment I entered the office. I scanned the agents' faces for clues as to the condition of my cat, but they all wore the inscrutable poker face that was common among lost baggage professionals.

Without a word, an older agent led me to the back room. There, on a table, sat Mooshie's carrier. Dangling from the handle was an orange neon tag with the word REROUTED printed on both sides.

I picked up the carrier and immediately thought, *Nope. Too heavy. Wrong cat.* My heart sank. Someone had taken Mooshie and replaced him with one of those obese cats frequently pictured on humorous greeting cards.

"It isn't him," I mumbled. "He's small; not quite eight pounds. He's—" My voice broke. The agent sat me down so that I was at eye level with the carrier.

"Look," he said. "Look inside."

I did as I was told and found two yellow bug-eyes gazing back at me through the holes.

I fumbled with the door clasps which had been secured with plastic zip ties. The agent took a Swiss Army knife from his pocket and swiftly cut them away. Reaching in, I pulled out the cat I adored. None the worse for wear, Mooshie snuggled against me, making soft love chirps. The smell of his breath was strong enough to walk on.

Mystified as to why the carrier was so heavy, I peered

271

inside. Under a hill of shredded newspaper was a dry salami and a nibbled wedge of provolone. An untouched slice of prosciutto lay in the corner, the edges dark and curled.

A ragged piece of cardboard stuck out from under the prosciutto. I gingerly took it out and read:

Your cat shredded his destination tag and ate it. We gave him water and half a tuna sandwich. He ate the bread crusts and peed on the boss's jacket. He's a cool cat.
— The Baggage Dudes

I wish I knew what other adventures Mooshie had on his trip to New Jersey's lost baggage world with the Baggage Dudes, but all that really mattered as I held my purring cat was that he was safe and we were together.

*

Our old wooden dock stretched some twenty feet out into the bay. It sagged a little in a few places, but not enough to deter the variety of local species from regularly gathering there. This included Mooshie, who loved hanging out on the end to watch the fish.

Early one evening, I stopped working to watch a young bottlenose dolphin surface repeatedly six feet from where Mooshie sat. Whisker pads quivering, my cat churned out a series of sounds that ranged from meows and chirps to a warbling call. The dolphin came to the edge of the dock, rose out of the water, and looked directly at my cat.

The eight-pound cat and the two-hundred-pound dolphin silently surveyed each other. They must have formed a friendly telepathic connection in that first meeting, because after that the dolphin returned to our dock two or three times a week to look for Mooshie.

Another regular dock visitor was Ernie, the neighborhood Great Egret. The neighbors told me that the cottage's previous tenants were an elderly couple who fell into the bad habit of feeding Ernie hot dogs. As a result, the egret was overly friendly with humans, and thought nothing of approaching them for food.

Each day the bird would swoop down to fish among the thick tangle of mangroves that lined the shore on either side of the dock. Fascinated by the seabird's fluid slow-motion maneuvers while he stalked his unsuspecting prey, Mooshie always stopped whatever he was doing to give the egret his full attention.

Ernie would suddenly pierce the water and come up with a wiggling fish skewered on the end of his beak. Spreading his wings to their full five-foot span, he'd then fly off with his catch. If put into words, Mooshie's expression could only be translated as, *Wow! What a bird!*

Ernie's razor-sharp beak and his great height kept Mooshie at a distance at first, but over time the seabird and the feline grew comfortable with one another. It was an improbable friendship, and one that I should have discouraged.

Our idyllic cottage did not have air conditioning, which might have been the reason the rent was so low. Being the heat seekers we were, this presented no problem for my cat and me, though I admit we both enjoyed the cooling cross breeze that came off the water each evening.

On the hotter, more humid nights, I slept with the front door open and the screen door latched. Early one morning I was awakened by a knock at the screen door. Mooshie, always happy to greet visitors, ran to see who was there while I grappled with my robe.

"Who is it?" I called.

The knock came again—harder this time.

I went to the door, noting that Mooshie stood on his hind legs, his nose pushed against the screen. Thinking Joplin had come to call, I unhooked the latch and pushed the screen door open a few inches to let Mooshie out. That was when Ernie stuck his head inside, took a quick look around, and stepped into the cottage like he owned the place.

We regarded each other: I, awestruck—he, indignant. Translation: *Where's my hot dog?*

"It's illegal to feed you, my friend," I explained, keeping a wary eye on his beak. "The hot dog wagon left the station years ago, so go back outside and find a fish."

I made shooing gestures, but Ernie was determined. He took a few steps deeper into the cottage, heading in the direction of the refrigerator. Sensing my discomfort, Mooshie shifted into shepherd mode and herded the egret toward the screen door—which was now closed.

There was no room to get around the bird, so I went out the back, hustled to the front of the house, and held the screen door open. Knowing when he wasn't welcomed, Ernie stepped outside and gracefully sailed to the end of our dock.

That night, Mooshie began his usual nighttime routine of pressuring me to go to bed, but I was on a roll and didn't want to stop writing. I indicated my reluctance to retire by failing to react to his hard stare, then his snaky-slither onto my lap. The snatch and grabbing of my spectacles was harder to ignore.

I put him on the floor and tolerated several rounds of his pawing at my legs. Normally at this point, he would concede defeat and take refuge with his Mother Teresa blanket. Instead, he went to stand by the screen door which was latched with a simple hook and eye fixture. He meowed to be let out.

"It's late," I said. "Go lie down with Mother Teresa."

He paid me no heed. From the ease with which he jammed the top of his head against the bottom of the hook and popped it out of the eye latch, I got the impression this wasn't the first time he'd successfully let himself out.

He fled into the night, but he'd been so good about staying nearby that I wasn't worried. When he didn't return by the time I shut down the computer, I went searching for him in all the hidey holes he frequented. He was nowhere to be found. Leaving the screen door unlocked and propped open, I went to bed.

In my dream, I was running a marathon to the beat of a tapping noise that was coming from somewhere close by. The smooth pavement under my feet disappeared and was replaced by mucky puddles of decomposing fish which slowed me down to a crawl. I was further troubled by something tangled in my hair, but couldn't pull it out because my hands were covered in fish slime and I didn't want to get my hair dirty.

In the skewed logic of dreams, I thought that if I could get to the source of the tapping noise, the fish muck and whatever was in my hair would disappear and I could continue with the marathon.

I was about to discover the source of the noise when Mooshie bounded onto my chest and slapped me awake with his paw. I opened my eyes to find him staring down at me wearing a faintly worried expression that read as, *Is she dead?*

The tapping noise was coming from the somewhere near the end of my bed. Rising up on my elbows, the sight that greeted me was so unlikely that I questioned if what I was seeing was real or if I was still dreaming. There, standing on my printer, loomed Ernie cleaning his beak by whacking it against one side of the machine, and then the other. He was also pooping all over the printer's output tray.

Close to my ear, something generated a sound like a dog's squeaky toy and burrowed deeper into my hair. Exercising restraint, I fought the urge to fly out of bed and shake whatever creature it was out of my hair. When living in the tropics you quickly learn that if you suspect a living creature has become entangled in your silky locks, such as a poisonous amphibian or spider, you should never jump about and scream. *That* was the surest way to rile the thing in your hair into retaliating.

I lay perfectly still while Mooshie rooted through my tangled tresses. The squeaking picked up in volume and two scaled down North American tree monkeys—better known as squirrels—tumbled onto my pillow.

I lifted my head to take in the whole scene—the pooping tapping seabird, the cat with breath like a sewer leak, the squeaky baby squirrels—and closed my eyes.

The following conversation went something like this:

Me*:* "Mooshie! Did you bring all these animals in here?"

Mooshie: *Brrrpt!* (Translation: *Yup!*)

Ernie: *Grgrgrgrg* (Translation: *Where's the hot dog?*)

Me: "You're killing my printer!"

Twin squirrels in unison: *Squeak! Squeak!* (Translation: *Feed us!*)

Me (*yelling*): "This is not a zoo, dammit!"

Against my better judgment, I named the twin squirrels Wenckebach and Mobitz the Second. Their every-two-hour feeding schedule, not to mention the amount of time it took to stimulate the rodents to pee and poop, left me exhausted.

No more than forty-eight hours after the introduction of the twins, Mooshie carried home a baby raccoon (alive) and a mouse (dead). I buried the mouse and gave the raccoon a bowl of kibbles (big mistake).

Like a little kid who has learned an annoying new trick, Mooshie regularly began luring Ernie to the cottage and letting him in. Each time I would have to stop whatever I was working on and usher Ernie back to the mangroves.

I hit my limit when I discovered that I was spending most of my time and energy tending to Mooshie's Zoo. In due course I sat my cat down for a serious talk.

"You have to stop bringing home all these strays, Mooshie."

He lifted his head and gave me his innocent *Who me?* look.

"You've got a problem, pal. You're like the cat who loves too much. In psychobabble terms, you'd be known as a codependent rescuer. Cats are supposed to be only concerned about themselves. You're completely out of your depth with all this knight in shining fur stuff."

Mooshie looked appropriately concerned. *"Brrrpt?"*

"Yes, there is a way to fix it. Let me show you how I'm going to help you with this problem."

Much to my cat's delight, I acted out each member of his menagerie so he would know what I was talking about. I then held up the carrier and mimicked putting each animal in it and carrying it out the door and away.

Determined to return to our normal routine, I waited until Mooshie went down for his afternoon nap, then quietly packed up Wenckebach and Mobitz the Second for their one-way trip to the island's wildlife center. The baby raccoon that was forever standing outside my screen door wringing his little hands like a worried beggar presented another problem.

I originally planned on giving him to the neighbors around the corner who would have been glad to take him in, but changed my mind when I recalled an incident that took place a month after we'd moved into the cottage.

We'd already retired for the night when I heard a commotion out in the bay. I grabbed the binoculars and hurried to the end of our dock to investigate. Six yards out I saw a dolphin thrashing about in the churning water. As far as I knew, sharks never came into the bay, but I couldn't think of anything else that would be large enough to challenge a full grown dolphin.

The battle continued for a minute or two then stopped. Seconds later, the dolphin passed under our dock moving at a rapid speed. Right on its tail in hot pursuit was a smaller, roundish creature, though I could not make out what it was. Aided by the street lamp and binoculars, I followed the two trails for about twenty yards, at which point the smaller of the creatures branched off and headed for shore.

A figure like an oblong hassock emerged from the water, shook itself, and tore across the road. Not believing my own eyes, I gasped as the immense raccoon disappeared under someone's house.

I returned to the cottage to find Mooshie sitting on the porch anxiously chattering while he paced. From the way he jumped onto my shoulder and licked my face, it was clear he was as freaked out as I was by the incident.

The next morning, I drove to nearby Mote Marine Laboratories and explained to a marine biologist what I'd witnessed, hoping he wouldn't think I'd been hallucinating. To my surprise, he assured me that not only could Florida raccoons weigh up to thirty-plus pounds, but they did indeed swim underwater at a good pace and were known to attack dolphins and other marine life.

Again, who knew?

Not wanting to risk the chance our little masked beggar might grow to be an enormous dolphin-hunting menace, I added him to the wildlife center passenger list.

As far as Ernie went, there wasn't much I could do about his constant intrusions into the cottage other than to move the hook and eye door latch out of Mooshie's reach.

As Mooshie's interest in zookeeping dwindled, he contented himself with Joplin's company. For the next few months, life at our cottage was so peaceful that I let my guard down and fell into a state of complacency.

But, like nettlesome guests, disruption and chaos had our address, and it wasn't long before they returned to our cottage for another visit.

*

The day began like any other on our barrier island. The weather was lovely—a bit warmer than usual, but with a nice breeze. I ran my usual five miles, ate breakfast, then settled down to work.

Mooshie, on the other hand, was being weird. Reminiscent of a special ops commando sneaking into enemy territory, he crouched low as he crept from one corner of our three hundred and twenty square foot cottage to the other, his head swiveling as he went. I suppose this strange new behavior should have alerted me to the fact that something was amiss—either that or my cat was recalling our evening with Robin Williams and was giving improvisational comedy a try.

I didn't own a television, and because I didn't care to get sucked into the vortex of the world's bad news while I concentrated on writing, I hadn't listened to the radio for a week or more. I will admit the thought did cross my mind that Mooshie knew something I didn't, but that notion was murdered by the characters in my mystery thrillers who demanded I concentrate on them and the plot development, and not my eccentric cat.

By late morning the sky had turned charcoal gray and the wind picked up. The flashbacks to our time on Montserrat that *should* have rung bells, failed to appear. Only when I took a break for lunch did I become aware that the rain was coming down so hard, I couldn't see the dock—nor could I see Mooshie.

I knew he hadn't gone out; all the screens were intact, and the doors were locked. Following the Montserrat playbook of hurricanes and tropical storms, I searched under the bed and got a glimpse of two eyes, pupils big as saucers, staring out at me from deep inside the box springs. It was Montserrat déjà vu.

No sooner had I pulled Mooshie from between the springs, than the transformer down the block exploded, knocking out the power. I put my cat in his carrier and glanced out the front door. The dock, the road, and the front yard were under water. It was, to use the Florida vernacular, a real toad-strangler of a storm.

I unplugged my laptop, hunted around for a waterproof bag to put it in, and escaped out the back door with it in one hand, and the cat carrier in the other.

From prior experience, I knew that Gulf Drive, the main road to all three drawbridges, would be under water. I was sure that if I could maneuver the van—already up to its lug nuts in water—onto the walking path along the bay, I might be able to make it to the Cortez drawbridge less than a quarter of a mile away.

I'd driven/floated about three hundred feet when I came up behind a small motorboat holding a policeman with a megaphone. He seemed awed by the sight of us as if the van were the Loch Ness monster emerging from the depths of the bay. I briefly wondered if there was a law against driving on a walking path if it was under water.

Speaking into his megaphone, he told me to pull over, except there wasn't an "over" to pull to. Instead, I rolled down my window a few inches, just enough to see his face.

"What the hell do you think you're doing?" he demanded.

"I'm trying to get off the island."

"Evacuation orders have been in effect since yesterday afternoon. Why didn't you evacuate then?"

"I didn't know. I don't have a television and I haven't had the radio on for a week."

He made a face. "What are you—some kind of troglodyte?"

I never know why some things strike me as funny, but this policeman in his little boat calling me a troglodyte launched me into an attack of hard, wheezy laughter.

"This isn't a laughing matter, ma'am," he warned in a gruff cop-like voice. "The Gulf and the Bay are one body of water right now. Do you understand that you're in a very dangerous situation here?"

In answer, a tortured howl came from the back of the van.

The cop's eyes went wide. "What the hell was *that?!*"

Another paroxysm of laughter gripped me until I could scarcely breathe. "My cat," I wheezed.

"Jesus!" The cop wiped the rain out of his eyes. "It's like working in an insane asylum out here." He waved me forward. "Stay to the right and head for the front of the police station. I'll let you through the emergency entrance onto the drawbridge. Try not to use your brakes."

We made it safely off the island onto the mainland, though I had trouble keeping the van on the road—not so much on account of the wind or flooded streets, but because I couldn't stop laughing.

I switched on the car radio and learned that the hurricane had been downgraded to a severe tropical storm. I parked on a downtown side street to wait until the worst of it passed, and the Gulf had a chance to return to its seabed.

Mooshie stood on my lap, his front paws pressed against the side window as he watched the water rush past the car. Without warning, his chin began to tremble and his ears went flat against his head. Pupils wide, he made his chattery *keh keh keh* sounds.

I peered down into the water at the same moment a ten-foot-long alligator swam by the van, sailed through the stoplight, and turned onto the main street—just like every other Florida commuter hurrying to get home on a stormy day.

*

The Bay receded, taking our mailbox with it. The sun and blue skies returned, along with our dock and the ever-loyal Joplin, who took up her post on the front steps once again.

The storm must have brought with it an atmospheric antidote against lassitude, for Mooshie was inexplicably infused with an exuberance for life that was infectious. He slept less and filled his days hanging out on the dock with Ernie and the dolphin, and playing vigorous games of tag with Joplin.

Through simple feline to human contact, I caught the bug. I spontaneously started taking in a movie once a week, and when Kellie the vet tech asked if I wanted to join her monthly book club, the members of which were mostly veterinarians and SPCA people, I jumped at the invite.

Mooshie and I spent more time playing and cuddling and he no longer had to badger me into retiring at a reasonable hour. We settled into a nighttime routine wherein I read while he licked and scraped his toenails clean. He would then bat my book aside, sit on my chest, and stare at me. Neither one of us would blink for the longest time before he'd lower his head to give me a nose kiss then curl up in the space between my neck and shoulder.

I often wondered what was going on behind those gold eyes. What was he thinking as he stared through me like that? Was he simply in the moment, or was he taking stock of his life and reminiscing?

For my part, I was loving him, needing nothing more from him than to just be there, alive and purring. It is this image of us content and happy to be in each other's company that I took into the future, come what may.

·17·

I'LL BE SEEING YOU
IN ALL THE OLD FAMILIAR PLACES

"You become responsible, forever, for what you have tamed."
— Antoine de Saint-Exupéry, *The Little Prince*

In June of the following year, two of the four mysteries, *Pulse* and *Panic,* were in the bookstores. The third, *Paradox,* was completed and in the Bardo state of copyediting. The fourth, *Fatal Diagnosis,* was in the process of being written.

My anxiety over meeting deadlines had long since been replaced by a more serious concern—Mooshie's rapidly declining health. The Mystery Plague was now a persistent evil shadow that hung over us. On average, every eight to ten weeks we were pulled into the torturous nightmare of emergency vet visits, lab tests, hospitalizations and intravenous medications, recovery, and ultimately, relapse.

No matter how many tests were run, not one vet was

able to definitively diagnose what the M. plague was. Was it related in some way to his brush with death in Puerto Rico, or a virus he picked up in the tropical forests of Montserrat? No one had the answer.

On Thanksgiving, 1998, Mooshie was entering the ring for another round with the Mystery Plague. He'd gone through the initial stage of a few days of listlessness, and with his diminishing appetite, was sinking slowly into the next phase.

I'd left him for two hours to attend a Thanksgiving dinner with the SPCA book club folks. As I was leaving, my host insisted I take one of the three leftover sweet potato and marshmallow casseroles. I'm not a fan of sweet potatoes, and I have never understood the use of confectioneries in food other than desserts, but to be polite, I accepted the dish thinking that I would pass it on to my elderly next-door neighbors.

I returned home and was shaken to find that Mooshie had bypassed stage two of the M. plague and slipped into stage three. The sight of those opaque membranes covering his eyes sent me into the usual rescue mode. He declined the cooked chicken slurry I made and refused to swallow the few drops of water I squirted into his mouth.

Resolved to be at the vet's first thing in the morning, I crawled into bed and curled around my cat whispering words of encouragement and solace.

I awoke at four a.m. to the sound of crinkling aluminum foil, followed by audible chewing. Thinking the cottage had again been invaded by God-only-knew-what wild tropical species, I felt around for Mooshie, didn't find him, and snapped on the light.

On the kitchen table, crouched over the sweet potato casserole that I'd neglected to put in the refrigerator, was my cat, devouring the stuff like a hungry bear in a McDonald's dumpster. His whiskers and snout were smeared with gooey marshmallow residue and his mouth was full of orange sweet potato. Half the casserole was gone.

I reached for the dish, but Mooshie threw himself over it, making a series of old lady noises that resembled Yoda's cries of *Mine! Mine! Mine!*

Thrilled that he was eating, I left him to it and went back to bed.

Two hours later I awoke to a bright-eyed, afebrile Mooshie playfully batting my nose. At noon, he finished off the rest of the casserole with zeal.

Who would have thought a marshmallow and sweet potato casserole would play the role of *deus ex machina*?

I called my host to ask for the recipe and was horrified to learn that other than the sweet potatoes, the main ingredients were sugar and butter. It didn't matter—if he liked it, I'd make one every day.

For the next week I watched Mooshie like a hawk. I was just beginning to think we'd beaten the M. plague when his energy suddenly waned and an ominous shadow loomed over us like a dense fog. This time the usual sinking feeling that accompanied the onset of all of Mooshie's bouts of the illness was replaced by a menacing fear that forced me to drop the veil of hope and face reality.

One night he insisted on going out onto the porch with Joplin. He lay next to her making a high-pitched squeaky purr as if he were explaining something that was of utmost importance. Joplin listened for a spell, her ears twitching. When he quieted, the tortie began to groom him—something she'd never done before.

The next morning Mooshie went to the dock and sat close to Ernie. The bird did not move away, but remained still, the two of them gazing out at the bay. That afternoon my cat roused out of a sound sleep, ears twitching. He succeeded in pushing open the screen door and returned to the dock. An hour passed before the dolphin showed itself.

I happened to look up just as Mooshie draped his paw over the end of the dock. I grabbed my binoculars and waited for the dolphin to surface. Thirty seconds later, the bottlenose rose and tentatively pushed its rostrum under Mooshie's paw.

It occurred to me then that Mooshie was saying goodbye, and all his creatures sensed it. Still holding onto the tail of hope, I refused to acknowledge what I knew to be happening, and went about preparing the pureed chicken and water slurry that I would urge him to eat.

I wrapped him papoose-style in his Mother Teresa blanket. Sliding the tip of a feeding syringe between his teeth, I pushed in a small amount of the slurry and stroked under his chin until he swallowed. I was about to repeat the procedure when I became aware of his steady gaze. I held my breath and met his eyes. In them, I saw both pity and a serene resolve. His expression could not have been any more explicit in its meaning than if he'd spoken the words in plain English: *I am letting you do these things because* you *need to.*

Even the hardest of skeptics would not deny that he was pleading with me to love him enough to stop the grim tug of war that had been going on between us for far too long. His expression was not foreign to me. I'd seen it time and time again in the eyes of my dying patients as they begged us, the medical warriors, to stop the life-saving assault and let them peacefully slip away.

Under my fingers, my cat's ribs and spine felt like rows of small sticks and marbles. "Forgive me, Mooshie, but I'm not as brave as you are. I am afraid to be without you."

He continued to watch me, unblinking. Disappointed.

I put down the feeding syringe and lay his Mother Teresa blanket on the bed, smoothing out the wrinkles. When I leaned down to kiss him, he purred in appreciation of being left to follow his own path to its end.

By the next morning, he was barely responding. I drove to the veterinarians' office and handed him over to Mary, the vet I most trusted.

She took one look at my cat then met my eyes, her expression grave. Cradling Mooshie in her arms, she walked away without a word.

Anguished, I paced the waiting room, trying to convince myself Mooshie would pull through again. I prayed. I begged. I bargained. I made promises to a generic higher power I wasn't sure even existed.

It felt like an eternity before Mary reappeared, handed

me my cat, and motioned for me to follow her to her private office. She closed the door and faced me wearing the expression of someone about to carry out a difficult but necessary task.

"Mooshie's kidneys have shut down. I don't need to tell you what that means."

I looked away, acutely aware of Mooshie nuzzling my neck.

"We can make him comfortable," she continued, "but there's nothing more we can do. If there was, we'd be doing it."

Other than the feel of Mooshie's head against my neck, nothing seemed real—not the room, not Mary, and most of all, not her words. My heart was pounding out of my chest, and my throat was so tight, I couldn't talk. All I wanted was to take my cat and get out of there—anything to avoid facing the reality of the present moment.

Mary reached out as if to take my cat from me. "Let me put him to sleep now. You can be right here with him. I promise he won't feel a thing. He'll go to sleep and—"

Shocked, I backed away, feeling the same fear and panic I would have experienced if someone had threatened to kill me. "No, not now." I fixed my gaze on Mooshie. "There has to be something more you can do. Maybe another medication? One that's new or in trials?"

Mary sighed and took one of my hands in hers. "We have tried every medication available. Think of the hundreds of pills Mooshie has had pushed down his throat, and the countless bags of intravenous fluids he's endured, and all the injections, and the force-feedings. I believe he's held on as long as he has because he's concerned about *you*. You need to take that burden from him.

"He's fifteen years old and in renal failure. You would never allow one of your patients to suffer like this. In your books, you write about your disdain for families who let their loved ones suffer because they can't let go. Now is the time to practice what you preach."

"I know but—" I choked.

"But nothing," Mary said, her voice firm. "Animals know when it's their time to die. Mooshie *wants* you to let him go. He has had a good life, but I guarantee you he's not having a good time now. If you hope to show him how much you love him, let him have a dignified and painless death."

Hearing what I knew to be the truth, I buried my face in Mooshie's fur. I thought of the hundreds of times I'd said these very same words to my patients' loved ones. Tormented by the thought that Mooshie was suffering, I nodded.

"Take him home." Mary said. "Say goodbye. I'll give you fluids that you can administer to keep him comfortable. Day after tomorrow, I'll drive out to your cottage after work and—"

The sensation of warmth spreading down the front of my chest caused me to glance down. Mooshie had lost control of his bladder without being aware he'd done so.

I peered into my cat's eyes and saw his sincere desire for the release I knew I could no longer deny him.

*

The family around the corner had taken in Joplin as their own, but for those next two days, the tortie never left our porch. Each morning she peered through the screen door and mewed, letting Mooshie know she was there.

Using his Mother Teresa blanket, I created a nest for Mooshie on the bed and snuggled around him, getting up only to give him fluids or carry him to his litterbox. I spoke softly about the people whose hearts he'd touched, and reminded him of all the places we'd gone, and the experiences we'd had. I told him how grateful I was for the happiness he brought into my life. The more I talked, the closer I came to understand that this small, funny cat had been my greatest teacher in the art of unconditional love.

That last day, I tidied up the cottage and turned on the lights, then crawled back into bed with Mooshie, stroking his head while I held him close.

"You were the better half of us," I whispered. "You—"

Mary's car pulled into my driveway. I closed my eyes, willing myself to concentrate on love and gratitude.

Mary entered the cottage and briefly hugged me. "Are you ready?"

I hesitated, then nodded.

She squeezed my arm, letting me know she understood and placed her black leather case on the kitchen table. "I'll shave his leg first, and then I'll administer a sedative, quickly followed by a drug that will shut off his brain." She paused. "His heart will stop after that."

I forgot to breathe, remembered, and sucked in a breath.

"He won't be in any distress," Mary continued. "You can hold him the entire time."

Tenderly placing Mooshie on his Mother Teresa blanket, I wrapped my arms around his frail body. The soft buzz of the shaver was intrusive—too loud and too real. I took one of his paws between my fingers and massaged his pads the way he liked. We held each other's gaze, never breaking the connection.

"Thank you for being the best cat," I whispered. "Thank you for sharing your life with me."

The buzzing stopped. I flinched at the sound of a faint pop as Mary unsheathed the syringe.

Mooshie moved an inch closer to me, lowered his head, and licked my arm.

I kissed the top of his head and told him I loved him.

My extraordinary, unconventional cat closed his eyes and the light of his loving presence flickered and went out. His Mother Teresa blanket securely wrapped about him, I held him close and rocked.

When it was time, I opened all the doors and windows and let his soul fly free.

·EPILOGUE·

Mooshie hung around the cottage for about a year after his death. I'd occasionally catch the flick of his tail from the corner of my eye, or feel him jump up on the bed as I was drifting off to sleep.

Sometimes, as I wrote into the wee hours of the morning, I would hear his distinct *brrrpt* and feel the fleeting touch of his paw on my leg telling me it was time for bed. On more than one occasion I awoke to the sound of his snores and felt the weight of his soft body against my chest. I once caught a glimpse of him reflected in the mirror. That scared me enough to consider that I might be losing my mind. But, I reasoned, I'd rather be crazy and have Mooshie near me than be sane and not have him at all.

According to neurologist and author Oliver Sacks, these occurrences of seeing and experiencing the presence of a deceased loved one are common among those who lose a much-loved person or pet. Dr. Sacks assures us that these phenomena, known as bereavement hallucinations, are no more than the mind playing tricks

My apologies to the late Dr. Sacks, but I choose to believe they were real. I *wanted* Mooshie's ghost around. No matter if my sightings of him were tricks of the mind or not, they provided comfort.

Right after Mooshie's death, one of my ex-friends callously commented, "Maybe *now* you can return to living a normal life."

I did not move on to normalcy. Like my cat, I'd been an unconventional outlier since I was born; why would I want to be normal now? If I had "gone normal," Mooshie would have been disappointed.

At the news of his death, friends and fans wrote to extend their sympathies and relate their favorite Mooshie stories. My father recalled the day Mooshie experienced his first catnip high and promised to plant another catnip patch in Mooshie's memory as soon as the ground thawed.

Harry, Mooshie's bearded cat minder, sent an email:

> *Echo,*
>
> *I was sorry to hear about Mooshie's passing. The little guy was my first one-on-one cat experience, and because of him, I am now owned by three felines who run the house . . . and my life.*
>
> *My greatest fear was if Mooshie escaped and became pothole filler on my watch, my life would be worth spit. I remember the day I put him outside on his leash, and when I came back to get him, he was gone. I found him inside a blackberry bush. It took an hour to get him out. He was unscathed, I was*

bleeding like a stuck pig. I think it was Mooshie's way of getting rid of his human oppressor—if only he could save those magic opposable thumbs that operated the tuna can opener.

He was truly one of a kind. Harry

*

I know people who, upon losing a loved pet, buy or adopt a replacement pet within days to lessen their grief. I couldn't do that. What I did do was to throw myself into the two healing activities I knew best—writing and running.

In those first few months after Mooshie's death, my writing schedule bordered on the insane. I worked fourteen to sixteen hours a day, or until the text on the monitor began to blur. Even my characters began to question my mental health. Adele, the series' principal character, went on strike, taking the rest of the characters, including her dog, Nelson, with her.

Adding guilt to grief, my normal running pace was replaced by a frenetic rhythm as I raced to escape the "what ifs" that began to plague me. What if I hadn't dragged Mooshie to Puerto Rico and the West Indies? What if I'd put him in a kennel and not left him with Freddy Krueger? What if I'd kept him in a nice, normal house and maintained my quasi-normal job and a quasi-normal life instead of a nomadic, wild existence populated with poisonous amphibians, hurricanes, cat-hating islanders, and mountain lions?

It didn't take long to realize guilting myself was pointless. Eventually I shifted to a slower pace, giving myself time to meditate and reflect on the life of the small cat who had brought such love, comfort, and revelation into my life. Starting from the day we met, I thought of all the things he taught me about love and instinct and commitment—a slow miracle working inside my life, all just by being a cat.

In the way that life has of reminding us of those we loved when the pain of loss begins to wane, something will inevitably pop up to wrench them back into sharp focus. Like the time I gave the cottage a thorough spring cleaning and found one of Mooshie's toy mice neatly hidden in the box springs. I clutched the tattered toy as my initial laughter turned to sobs.

Once my well-meaning friends judged that I was ready, they urged me to adopt another cat. When I refused, these same friends threatened to bring me a cat. In response, I was forced to use my harshest truck driver language skills to assure them it would not be in their best interest to follow through with *that* flawed plan.

As I write these words, I am sorry to say that in the twenty-two years since Mooshie's death I have not been owned by another cat, although for a few years I did have meaningful connections with felines of a different sort.

A year after Mooshie died, I returned to California and took up residence in a small cabin in a national park. Because of my remote location and my preference for running off the beaten track, I soon discovered that I was living among established populations of mountain lions and bobcats.

The first indication I had of their presence came one icy January morning as I was running an old trail that would take me to the Pacific Ocean. I was so lost in my thoughts that I almost missed the red and pink blob in my path. I slowed just enough to recognize the scant remains of a rabbit. The kill was so fresh, bits of intestine were still steaming. *Coyotes hunting in daylight hours?*

Picking up my pace, I puzzled over what animal might have been hunting in that part of the park. A hundred yards on, I rounded a tight bend at speed and skidded to a dead stop inches from the hindquarters of a large male mountain lion.

I went rigid, motionless as a granite pillar.

The cat, on the other hand, casually looked over his right shoulder wearing the same apathetic expression I'd often seen on Mooshie's face whenever he was bored and tired.

For the two seconds we remained fixed in place, I was acutely aware of the tip of his lengthy tail brushing against my shin. The image that immediately came to mind was the Ojai mountain lion heading for Mooshie. Without any forethought, I mimicked Mooshie's come-play-with-me call.

Unimpressed, the mountain lion idly sauntered away. Later, when my legs stopped shaking, the only explanation I had for the cat's unnaturally lackadaisical attitude was his belly full of rabbit snacks. Then again, it could have had something to do with the cat's familiarity with the one and a half million visitors who swarmed the park each year.

After that I was always on the alert, keeping detailed records of the locations of markings, scat, and tracks. I had occasional sightings of two mountain lions—the male I'd run into, and a female that hung out near the creek that ran through the park. I never saw them in the same territory, let alone together, but the last time I saw the female, she was trailed by two cubs.

The bobcats were a different story. I would sight them at least twice a week and soon came to recognize certain individuals in the clutter. My presence did not seem to bother them in the least. The bobcat that I ran into most often actually approached me once, sat down about twelve feet away, regarded me for a few seconds, then laid down and rolled onto his back. It was exactly what Mooshie used to do when he wanted smack snack treats.

And although the park's animal biologist tried to dissuade me from running in these areas, the park service did make use of my records when placing their wildlife cameras.

*

My next move took me back to Florida. It was there, in a quiet cul-de-sac near the Gulf of Mexico that I was adopted by Maxwell, a Maine Coon with whom I fell in love.

Max invited himself into my house one day, liked what he smelled, and decided then and there that I belonged to him. Resolved to make me love him, Max made my house his own, even though he already had a home with a remarkable young couple who lived one house down from me. Cat people to the max—no pun intended—they understood that Maxwell had bestowed upon me the honorable role of Grandma, and gave him free rein to come and go between our two homes whenever he liked.

As it turned out, he liked hanging out with me a lot.

Max was so skilled in the art of rescuing lost humans who were stuck in the realm of the catless heartbroken, I was sure he was working for the APCH, Animals for the Prevention of Cruelty to Humans. Through his persistent affection and trickster's antics, he charmed his way through the fear that I would never be able to open my heart to another cat.

Once I was under his spell, Max would sometimes glance my way wearing a crooked smile that said, *"See? You* can *love again. All is not lost.*

Max convinced me that somewhere there is an outlier cat who will adopt me as his own and invite me to love him. He will teach me things I would never know without him, and show me wonders I would not see on my own.

I can hardly wait to meet him and experience that moment of recognition when I'll know that I have been chosen.

ACKNOWLEDGMENTS

Publishing a book is never a one-person operation. There are always others involved who help make the finished product as good as it can be. Thus, my deepest gratitude goes to the following:

Simon Heron—for the patience you showed your "special needs" pseudo-brother.

Joni Frasson and Jaspurr—for making Mooshie a part of your family, and for your wonderful photos of him.

David Neseralla—for loving the "Mooshmeister" almost as much as I did, and for allowing him to sleep on your face.

Frank Langben—as always, for your great catches and astute suggestions during my overly long process of getting this book out.

Kathleen "Comma Slayer" McClure—for your attention to detail. Your hilarious comments kept me laughing throughout.

Kellie Marx—vet tech extraordinaire, for always being on the lookout for another cat to own me.

Kelly Pratt—for your kindness the night Mooshie died.

Lauren and Jared Gould—for your wisdom in rescuing Baby Max, and for your generosity in sharing him so that he could rescue me.

Baby Max—for fostering me and stealthily working your way into my heart to heal the grief that lingered there.

Steven Vermillion, my husband, for urging me to finish this book. Thank you for your words of comfort when memories of the cat who once owned me, began to bite.

ABOUT THE AUTHOR

Echo Heron is the New York Times bestselling author of *Intensive Care: The Story of a Nurse* and nine other books including *Condition Critical, Mercy, Tending Lives,* and the Adele Monsarrat mystery series: *Pulse, Panic, Paradox, and Fatal Diagnosis.*

Ms. Heron's more recent works include *Noon at Tiffany's: An Historical Biographical Novel,* and *Emergency 24/7: Nurses of the Emergency Room.* They are available online and in all formats.

Ms. Heron lives with her husband in Northern California where she continues to write obsessively.

Made in the USA
Las Vegas, NV
17 January 2022

41667463R00187